Full Circle

JANET BAKER

Full Circle

An Autobiographical Journal

WITH PHOTOGRAPHS BY ZOË DOMINIC

Julia MacRae

A DIVISION OF FRANKLIN WATTS

First published in Great Britain 1982 by
Julia MacRae
A division of Franklin Watts
8 Cork Street, London, W1X 2HA
Published in the United States of America by
Franklin Watts Inc.
387 Park Avenue South, New York 10016

Designed by Douglas Martin
Set in 'Monophoto' Ehrhardt
Printed in Great Britain by BAS Printers Limited,
Over Wallop, Hampshire
Bound by Hunter & Foulis Limited, Edinburgh

British Library Cataloguing in Publication Data
Baker, Janet
Full circle.
1. Baker, Janet, 2. Opera – Biography
3. Singers – Biography
I. Title
782.1′092′4 ML420.B/

UK ISBN 0-86203-107-9
US ISBN 0-531-09876-1

For my husband Keith
and for my parents

Contents

Acknowledgements

I would like to express my thanks to the Managements of the three opera companies, The Royal Opera, English National Opera, and Glyndebourne Festival Opera, for their kindness in allowing photographs to be taken for this book. I would also like to thank the following: the designer, Douglas Martin; Zoë Dominic and Catherine Ashmore; Paul Hirschman, who has compiled the list of my operatic roles which appears at the end of the book; Joanna Huddy, for help with typing the manuscript; Harold Rosenthal; my publisher, Julia MacRae, and her team. But most of all I wish to record my gratitude to my colleagues: this book is about their work as much as it is about mine.

List of illustrations

Introduction

I suppose people would call me one of the lucky ones. It's perfectly true. I am. I have all the things which, to the outward eye, spell 'success'. A marvellous career, the kind any performer dreams about, totally satisfying and fulfilling; a long and very happy marriage to the kindest man in the world who is not only a husband but a highly efficient business partner as well, a man who has run my life and looked after me in a way that is rare in ordinary marriages, never mind a 'show business' one; two utterly loving and understanding parents who backed me to the hilt in my decision to become a professional singer; my family, and a few close friends.

All my working life I have tried to avoid labels and maintain an image which transfers equally between all aspects of performing – the stage, the concert platform, the recital field; I have been able to achieve this, with the result that my repertoire and my musical experiences have been wide and rich. For what more could one possibly ask? Absolutely nothing. Not only am I an extremely lucky human being but I *know* this to be so.

As we reach certain mile-stones in life it is a natural thing to do some stocktaking, to step back from activity and evaluate one's situation both personally and professionally. Many people do this at the age of forty. As I approach fifty it seems to me a good idea to make some sensible plan of action in order to deal properly with the greatest traumatic event as an adult – retirement from public life. I have been a public figure for twenty-five years; the pressure has grown steadily more concentrated as the time has passed. It is not an easy thing, especially for someone like me who, regardless of the impression I may give during performance, is an intensely home-loving, private and in many ways introvert person. I have never longed for the bright lights, fame, or the drug of audience acclaim. Although these are part and parcel of the job, they have no reality for me. To stand up in front of strangers and bare my innermost soul has been agony to me; equally painful to face public judgement with courage.

I have sustained a certain measure of sanity by keeping at the forefront of my mind the sole reason for being a performer – that I believe my voice and power of communication through music were given to me by God, to be shared with others. This I have tried to do, but it has been with a sense of duty rather than of joy. Recently, through the help of close friends and of one friend in particular, Margaret Sampson, I myself have come to understand and participate in the joy of performing. This is something new to me, and in the sense that I have been relieved both of responsibility for the end result and of the terrible fear which has dogged me all my life, it is a miracle. I have reached a point where I feel myself to be an empty vessel. There must always be a personality involved in any human action, but I now stand out there, silent within, and allow the music to speak through me. It used to worry me greatly that there are always people in an audience who are unmoved, unreached, by what I do; I have always wanted *everyone* to understand my own particular message. Now, I realise that this is simply not my concern. All I have to do is prepare myself musically, physically, and psychologically for a performance, and then stand aside to allow the music to speak for itself. It is interesting to notice from audience reaction in a hall, from people's words to me afterwards, and from letters received through the post, that the reaction I now produce is much more violent than before. Those 'for me' are more so, those 'against' likewise. I see this as an extremely positive situation.

I am able, therefore, because of the experience I have just described, to take a look at my life with a real measure of peace, equilibrium, dispassion, call it what you will. The first thing that strikes me is that I am getting tired more quickly. I know that during these final years I must somehow conserve my strength, and it is obvious to me that my stage appearances take more from me physically than my other work. The season of 1981–82 was not planned specifically with any significant end in view. It just so happened that Covent Garden decided to put a new *Alceste* into their repertoire and asked me if I would do the title role. Then the English National Opera decided to revive *Mary Stuart* at the Coliseum, and Glyndebourne to do a new production of *Orfeo*, but all three works were arranged some years ago, as is usual. When I began to look at the diary for the year in question I realised that my work was in some strange way coming full circle. I would be appearing in one season at all the houses with which I had been involved over the years, with the exception of Scottish Opera. I had a sudden gut reaction to make it the final year for my stage work, and thereafter spare my energies for concert work. As soon as I made this decision I knew it was the right one.

'The season' in my terms begins in September and ends, well, whenever I get a holiday, which sometimes doesn't happen at all! In September 1981 I obeyed a strong impulse to write down my thoughts, starting with the new production of *Alceste*, and finishing with the last performance of *Orfeo* the following July. The only realistic way to do this was in the form of a diary. I have had many requests to write my autobiography, but always refused because I think it is too early to sum up my life, and I am not interested in pursuing the usual autobiographical form. Instead of the story of a life-time, which a reader would expect of an autobiography, I wanted to put one year of my life under a microscope, so to speak, because this particular year would be the last of its kind; other incidents crept in by themselves, demanding to be put into words.

All my seasons have been like the one I have written about, that is, a mixture of opera, concerts, recitals, and travel. The pattern is totally familiar to me, so are the opera houses and concert halls of which I write. Everybody's life is repetitious, including a performer's. Never having kept a diary before I could not write an account of my entire life with integrity, because I simply cannot remember the details. Singers are rather like actors in a way. We meet together as a group, work together, create together, then break up and disappear, perhaps never again to meet up with exactly the same team. When one is deeply involved in a common project, nothing which has happened before, or which will happen afterwards, has any reality. When something is over, it is over for good; one walks away from it towards another beginning. But really, all life is precisely like that. We begin again, we get a new chance, not only when we awake each morning but at each new moment of the day. That is why my decision to quit opera is, for me, a new beginning, rather than the ending that others have tried to make of it. I am leaving the stage on the early, rather than the late, side, but I am preserving the years I have left in order that I may still sing well until the final moment. I do not know when that will be. It doesn't matter. All that matters is that there is an abundance of wonderful music to be heard and there will always be enough performers around to make it live.

Part One

Alceste, Covent Garden

ALCESTE

Tragédie-Opera in three acts
French libretto by F. L. G. Gand Lebland du Roullet
after the original Italian libretto by Raniero de'Calzabigi
after Euripides
Music by Christoph Willibald Ritter von Gluck
Producer John Copley
Scenery Roger Butlin
Costumes Michael Stennett
Lighting Robert Bryan
Choreography Ronald Hynd
First night of a new production at the
Royal Opera House, Covent Garden
26 November 1981

Le Héraut	Philip Gelling
Évandre, confident	Maldwyn Davies
Alceste, Reine de la Thessalie	Janet Baker
Le Grand Prêtre	John Shirley-Quirk
L'Oracle	Matthew Best
Admète, Roi de la Thessalie	Robert Tear
Le Dieu Hercule	Jonathan Summers
Un Dieu Infernal	John Shirley-Quirk
Le Dieu Apollon	Philip Gelling
Coryphées	Elaine Mary Hall, Janice Hooper-Roe, Mark Curtis, Matthew Best

The Royal Opera Chorus
Chorus Master: John McCarthy
Orchestra of the Royal Opera House
Conductor: Charles Mackerras

Ron, head of Covent Garden wig department, came over to fit my Alceste wig and bring me up to date on all the Opera House gossip! We fortified him with a bowl of Keith's gorgeous home-made soup and after half an hour I felt I had caught up on the news since my last appearance in the house [*Idomeneo.* 1978]. The gossip wasn't in the least unkind, just amusing and terribly to the point. Ron is the first person to greet the news of my final year in the theatre with enthusiasm. He thinks my decision is a really great idea! Not, I truly believe, because he feels I'm over the hump, but because he has seen a number of artists at close quarters who, either for reasons of health or vocal decline, should have given up earlier. It causes everyone such anguish to see a respected colleague somehow muddy a lifetime of marvellous work. Relating a story about one beloved singer, whom he literally nursed through a performance after a heart attack in the dressing-room during the first interval, Ron rolled his eyes at me and said a heartfelt, 'Never again'. I think he's glad for me to be taking the step early rather than late.

Keith and I lunched with a soprano friend and her husband and the conversation turned to the recent performance of another illustrious artist. With perhaps one exception, the press praised this concert. Our hosts, who had heard it, were broken-hearted to witness the failing powers of a glorious singer; so were a number of people who spoke to me of it later. Yet the public had gone wild at the end of the evening. How is anyone able to make a clear-sighted judgement about retirement when both press and public conspire to blur the truth and even encourage us to go on beyond reasonable limits? It is one of the hardest decisions to reach, perhaps the hardest of all, but it *must* be considered dispassionately by the person most deeply con-

I

cerned. Neither public nor press tell us the truth. It is a personal decision and we usually get it wrong.

Sussex for the day to choose a flat for the Glyndebourne period next summer. There will be no time for us to spend on house-hunting once this month is over, so we all went down and met Janet Moores (who was at Glyndebourne my first year there). She looks older, of course, but familiar; as does Lewes and the surrounding country, achingly so. I didn't think of the intervening productions since my chorus years, *Dido*, *Calisto*, *Ulisse*; just of those first two years, 1956–57; sharing digs with a girl who had an enormous, dark, Verdian voice of great beauty, plus burning ambition but definitely not the temperament to go with it.

The first season was a total revelation to me. I suddenly 'discovered' the world of opera and it seemed a hot-bed of intrigues, passion, and the struggle to come to terms with a genius, Carl Ebert, a god with feet of clay. I watched all this from the sidelines of ignorance and a weight problem of eleven stone three! The hardest thing to understand was the greatness of Carl Ebert. I expected a genius to be god-like in every way but his rehearsals revealed him to be all too human, particularly when working with a lesser talent or a singer he just didn't like. I remember Peter Gellhorn, our wonderful chorus master, gently trying to explain to me that tremendous talent usually *was* wrapped up in very human packages with all that this implies. In the twenty-five years since Peter's wise and kindly words I have worked with many people of genius and have learned not to expect the parcel to be as perfect as the talent it hides; thank God!

We have chosen a tiny, compact, easy-to-run flat right on the sea-front. I can imagine Keith and me walking there next June, late at night with a brisk wind blowing, while I rant and rave about the trials of the day's rehearsal!

2

First costume fitting at the wardrobe department of Covent Garden.

My first act Alceste design is magnificent in both colour (old gold shining through black) and shape (draped pleats). But oh! it is heavy. Michael Stennett, the excellent designer of *Werther* and *Julius Caesar* at the 'other place', has tried his very best to make it light knowing that heavy garments aggravate my weak back. Wearing something for a solid hour and lifting one's arms in invocation to the gods is no joke, and can't be compared with the weight of a length of cloth held in the hands for a few moments. Michael is utterly understanding though and will try to cut some yardage off the train. They all stand round me in a circle, Gabriella, who has made the costume, jewellery-maker, shoe-maker and assistants. It is a democratic process. I make suggestions, they make suggestions; Michael is good about compromise and as I am slowly pinned and cut something emerges which is going to look superb. After an hour and a half carrying the weight even without wig or the head-dress, I am exhausted. I look at myself in the huge mirror. I should be thinking: How marvellous! A new production of a great opera in this house. I should be feeling stirred with excitement at the prospect. But I feel nothing except deep relief that this is the last time in my life I shall stand here in the early stages of fitting and that I shall be free of the bone-tiredness such a session entails, free for good. The conviction arises yet again, how right I am in the decision to put aside this aspect of my work which takes so much from me in purely physical terms. During the past two months of blissful holiday there has been so much to do; days filled with the interest of so-called 'ordinary' things which are so 'extra-ordinary' to me. The chains which bind me with such total commitment to my profession are loosening their grip. Day after day this summer I have wakened in the morning without that sickening lurch in the stomach which tells me 'This is a performance day.' I have visited new places seen with an

3

unfamiliar clarity because I have been there without a performance hanging over my head. One day, all my experiences will have this clarity, this freedom from responsibility; I shall take journeys and be able to look at the country instead of burying my head in yet another new score. I think of it with nothing but joy.

Thursday
1 *October –*
Morning
Bob and Jonathan come to talk about the television film they hope to make, covering my last three operas during the season. They are touchingly enthusiastic and feel a tremendous sense of responsibility to get my final year of opera on record. I appreciate this, deeply, but am at the same time detached about the project. If it happens, O.K. If they can't get the finance, well, that will be too bad. They have many good suggestions about how to relieve me from too much stress; it will be a strain, undoubtedly; I must try not to feel hampered in rehearsal by the thought of my every word and action being put onto film. Rehearsals are the greatest possible joy because they are private; there will be little privacy for me this year if the scheme comes off. The boys are going to fit small microphones onto us instead of using a sound boom; this will certainly help. I also have right of veto.

Thursday
1 *October –*
Afternoon
Photograph session at Zoë Dominic's studio; all my favourite pictures during the last twenty-five years have been hers. This session is most unusual; a costume for a new production is rarely complete before the final piano dress rehearsal and even then modifications are necessary right up to the last moment. But here complete is my beautiful black and gold dress, a loose, pleated robe with wide sleeves, together with its jewellery, wig and crown. The wig needs a little more experiment, they always do, but for a first try it looks terrific and very natural. The photographs are to

4

be used for a poster which is to be printed almost immediately, hence the hurry. I stand there for three and a half hours trying to get some life and sense of the character as Zoë shoots away with cries of 'Wonderful, darling. That's divine. Oh, beautiful!' It is hard, hard work and I am dropping by the end of the afternoon. Fortunately, this sort of strain has been planned well before the rehearsals begin. From 26 October I go into musical purdah.

My friend Edward Boyle died this week. I thank God his suffering is over. A greater friend to music and to musicians never lived. I saw him when he was still the Edward we all knew, respected and deeply loved. I did not want to see the skeleton he became during the last weeks, although even last November he was a sight to break the heart. It hurt to see him so small and thin; it hurt even more to watch that mind of his no longer able to concentrate. He was summed up in a two column obituary which made him seem a slight failure! Such a man; such a contribution, reduced to a few uninspired words. He will soon be forgotten, except by a few. We are all soon forgotten; five minutes after I walk off the platform for the last time, I shall be forgotten. This thought helps me so much in my decisions to time it all exactly right if I possibly can. To stop performing is a kind of death. It is important to die well. Mary Queen of Scots managed it superbly!

Thursday   Manchester for the first two concerts of the new season. *Nuits*
8 October   *d'Été* with Jimmy Loughran and the Hallé. We had absolutely marvellous rehearsals, pure self-indulgent joy; why do we have to have an audience? The concerts were almost as good though. The orchestra gave me the sort of accompaniment one dreams about and we all made music together. After I had finished singing, I heard one of the first violins say, 'Brava. Smashin'.' I'd rather have that sort of praise than a rave review in *The Times* any day.

6

Tuesday My first music call on *Alceste*. For a whole year I have lived with
13 *October* this score; at home, on journeys; now I shall see if she is truly in
my bones. Alceste, wife of the dying Admetus, King of Thessaly,
makes a pact with the god Apollo that she will die in her
husband's place. Admetus refuses to allow this and the opera is
about the struggle of wills between husband and wife which
Alceste eventually wins. She is taken to Hades but is rescued by
Hercules and restored by Apollo to her husband Admetus.

Floral Street is a dark tunnel just now because of building work
going on. I walked the short distance from the Underground
station to the stage door asking myself the question, 'What do you
feel, then? This is the last time you will ever walk to a first music
call on a new production for this house!' I waited for the sky to
fall on my head. Nothing happened. Last times. There will be
many such moments during the year. So far there is nothing but
relief. No nostalgia; no regret. Maybe I am riding for a great big
fall and the enormity of it all will hit me very soon. The complete
absence of churning in my solar plexus is gratifying though.
Maurits Sillem took me right through the score in a tiny room
with a low ceiling and a lousy piano. I wanted to sing out fully in
order to test my stamina. Rehearsal conditions are much tougher
vocally than singing the entire opera because I get no rests in
between scenes and acts. I wondered if I would manage it but
when Keith picked me up afterwards I felt in great form and my
speaking voice, usually affected by hard singing, was quite
normal. Perhaps I am going to be able to sing the role, after all!
We had a brief lunch down in the bowels of the canteen and saw
many old friends; everyone is so NICE to me.

Sunday My final concert (recital at Charterhouse) before really getting
18 *October* down to *Alceste*. Now I don't have to keep any music in my head
other than the opera, at least until mid-December. What a
luxury!

7

Monday
19 October We spent the day clearing the decks – in other words, planning programmes for the American recital tour in January. Any minute now the Shaw office, my agents in the United States, will be writing for my programmes, plus all the texts and translations to print. The job has taken me from noon today until 6.30 p.m. but it is done and again is something else off my mind.

Norwich

Tuesday
20 October Dear Dame Janet,

My wife and I, who have been your devoted fans for many years, are very sorry to hear of your impending retirement . . . etc., etc., etc.

Dear Mr . . . ,

Thank you for your letter. I was touched by your very kind words. I am not retiring in 1981. I have just decided not to do any more opera after July next year. I hope to go on singing for some time yet. Etc., etc., etc.

Wednesday
21 October Things are hotting up. The hardest day so far, starting with a marvellously exhilarating morning. I had Janine Reis on a French session. Since she is not only the most inspiring language coach imaginable but also a first-rate pianist, we made great strides forward. Picking the bones of recitative apart; judging the tempo of each phrase, deciding on the words which need more stress, those which need less, is exciting work. The music staff have always told us that it is in the singing of recitative that the true test of the great singer, and the ability to bring a character to life, really lies. Anyone can sing an aria. Few people can employ heart and imagination in bars of sung speech.

We had the camera crew in the room, but after they had fixed our mikes we were genuinely able to forget about the film-making and enjoy two hard hours of work, tossing ideas about and trying

8

them out for size. Working with a microphone stuck down my chest and a camera following every move is like giving a master class in public – a master class with myself as both teacher and guinea-pig. The character comes nearer and nearer. I am aching to employ the final act of creation – the physical movement – but that moment will arrive next week. Surprisingly, again, I did not feel tired at the end of our rehearsal, just terribly excited by the things we had discussed. Janine is very complimentary about my singing of her language. In the middle of the session she got up from her piano-stool, hugged me, and said, 'Oh! it is marvellous to be working with you again.' Remarks like this from real experts mean so much to me. Bob seemed pleased with the film and we all separated, I to a series of interviews which left me feeling as though I knew quite a lot more about the interviewers than they did about me! The real fatigue didn't hit me until we were in the car driving home. I went straight to bed and had my supper there, relishing the peace and the fact that talking was done for the day.

Almost forgot: saw Gabriella in the canteen at lunch-time. She caught my eye and said, 'I've got some interesting material for you to see when you've a moment to spare.' I made one in between lunch and the first interview. She handed me a large paper bag and said, 'There, that's your Act II costume.' It felt as light as a feather, gorgeous white material with a discreet silver thread running through it. Wonderful!

These are my final three days of freedom before I begin several weeks as a commuter. We have cut our grass for the last time this year. I have answered my letters, got my clothes cleaned, bought my Christmas cards, and paid all the visits I owe.

Sunday
25 *October*   I am not a singer; I am a human being who happens to sing. In bed all day with a terrible migraine and sickness.

9

Monday Everyone met today. After a concentrated morning music
26 October session with producer, conductor, coach, and tenor colleague,
my Alceste is reduced to a wreck. She lies around my feet in
shattered fragments. Everyone else has got hold of her and she is
totally lost to me: the next weeks will be the process of putting
her back together again. She is a muddle of beats in a bar and
different view-points and this is even before I have taken a single
step. Tomorrow, when I use my body, things may seem a little
better. I must not, *will* not, forget that I know her better than
any of them. What I superimpose of their ideas is only an outer
shell. She really lives and breathes only through me. I shall hold
on to that. As soon as I move, the timing, the words and
emotions she must speak will begin to assert themselves strongly.
There is a tremendous struggle between written notes, the
mathematical values, and those of heart and soul. Somehow, I
have to find a connecting bridge between the two and it will not
be easy. I think this has been the hardest and least rewarding first
day I've ever known with a new production. Yet it is a wonderful
team.

Tuesday The world is the right way up again. I wonder if the strangeness
27 October of yesterday was due to the fact that I was recovering from the
bad migraine on Sunday? Charles Mackerras, tough though he
is, must have been suffering also, from jet-lag, as he only returned
from Australia at the weekend. So did Bob Tear. And John Copley
from America. Anyway we had a good morning of music, then
parted for lunch. I saw some colleagues in the canteen and had a
happy time, they made me laugh so much. I have known John
Dobson since my early twenties; a kinder or more professional
person doesn't exist. If he's asked, he always gives tactful, helpful
and valuable advice; life must have been good to him because his
sense of humour hasn't turned grey with his hair!

At last – we are acting. Even the dreaded London Opera

With Maurits Sillem (centre) and Charles Mackerras

Centre seems inviting; the set is there in embryo, at least the different levels exist and the entrances. The music has suddenly slotted into the proper place. We got completely through the first scene in one session, remarkable! Charles is compromising with me more and more and I with him. John Copley has us safely controlled by his own wonderful brand of unending patience. I have worked with a very small number of producers and they have all understood me enough to give me a fairly free rein. John came up the hard way, learning the business in the opera house itself. He comes totally prepared with a deep and true feeling for the music, a genius in dealing with large numbers of people. He never wastes a moment, and makes his singers believe it's all coming from us. But of course it isn't; his way of quietly and unobtrusively describing the feelings we should have in just a few words fires the imagination, and the acting comes from somewhere totally natural. I think his secret, with me at any rate, is to give me so much confidence in my ability that he creates the circumstances for anything to happen just because he makes me believe it can!

Oh! what a relief to go home, so tired but with a solid piece of work done in an atmosphere of friendliness and enjoyment. I pray I keep well. To wake up feeling as I did on Sunday morning, unable to lift my head from the pillow, is frightening. The one thing I can't control is my body. All my life I have been able to keep functioning on will-power, often singing when no sane person would have done. But now, the voice is more and more affected by the way I feel physically and no amount of determination is enough to support the sound when I am under par.

Wednesday
28 October

The L.O.C. awash with people. Dancers twirling away in corners, actors standing patiently waiting, chorus members knitting, reading; they are waiting too. All the music staff, all the production staff, are sitting facing us in a long line. A morning like this really generates excitement. Sheer numbers raise not only the physical temperature but the emotional one as well. We all react on one another and suddenly for minutes at a time, some of the magic settles on the cast and the huge ugly space becomes theatre.

There is a lot of laughter and hard work. A few of the chorus were with me in the Glyndebourne chorus. Two of the actors were my generals in the recent *Julius Caesar* production at the Coliseum; the chorus-master, new to Covent Garden since I was last here, is an old friend – John McCarthy – who gave me freelance chorus jobs in the Ambrosian Singers many years ago. Mac knows more about the business and the individual way it works than anyone else I know.

In the afternoon, rather fewer people; Bob Tear and I start working together. Somehow we have to find a way to convince an audience that we are two people who would literally die for one another. We have to find it in four weeks. He is so good to have as a partner – a fine singer and an actor who looks you between the eyes, a most difficult thing to do. Most singers fix the eye just above the eyes of the person they are supposed to be looking at. This does not work. The eyes must have true contact in order to spark off emotion; the final depths cannot surface until we have the help which sets, lights, and costumes bring. The main stumbling-block is the necessity to keep going in and out of the emotion to re-map a move. With the inevitable stops and starts, one can't get a 'run' at the scene. That will come later. But the basic ingredients are there. Also, at the moment I am 'marking' – singing *sotto voce* – sparing the instrument as much as I can. With the chorus this morning, I found I had to sing out to them, in order to make them reach out to me. As soon as I sang at them, they began to give me back an extraordinary amount of feeling; when we approach the final days this will heighten and help me enormously. It is such team-work, never the sole responsibility of one person.

13

With Robert Tear

Friday A wonderful day. Very quiet; just John, Janine, and a small
30 October group of assistants, Bob and me. We really got down to second
act details, stopping at every line in order to understand in depth
what is being said. If this work is not done at the deepest levels
the outer layers of our portrayals will not work. When we
understand and feel in depth, the extent of our exploration
affects the superficial acting, and although perhaps not apparent
to anyone but us, stamps our Alceste and Admetus with a quality
which would not otherwise be there. The deeper we go, the less
there is to do with gesture and 'outside' effect. The interior work
is so true, one needs to do nothing – in other words, the body
moves because of the inner thought. It is a complete reflection of
the mind and heart.

We spend all day on one scene, trying again and again to
establish the incredible connection between these two people.
We have to believe in them; the quality of the score becomes
more and more apparent and as in all great music the answer to
each problem lies in the printed score. The arias sing themselves
but the wideness of choice in the recitative, the pacing, the
dynamics, which can be so personal, nevertheless impose on the
singer a certain nobility of style; if one ignores this, the words
become 'modern' and lack significance, especially if the
statement is fast and vigorous. We are discovering a trick of
singing the fastest notes, i.e. those of the smallest value, with a
sort of deliberation, and we are articulating the consonants
clearly, so that a kind of natural braking effect comes into
operation. This gives the phrases the right feel and they still
sound fast, but at the same time noble. I have noticed when
singing Debussy or Ravel that these two composers write music
in a way which, if obeyed implicitly, solves the problem of
singing the French language; and they both give importance to
syllables which in English would be unimportant or thrown
away; words like *the, of, and*.

I spend the entire lunch-hour talking to Bob Bentley about

15

filming details; the day disappears effortlessly. This always happens when one is totally absorbed and interested. It is boredom which slows down time.

The cast was not called; Janine and John came over to my house instead to work on my Act I arias. 'We're going to do some digging today,' John said, peering at me through his spectacles. He didn't mean the gardening variety either! For two hours we sweated in my music room, working through the recitatives, word by word. 'I want you to feel every emotion for real from now on. Everything you do and say has to come from the right place, there is to be no easing up at all.' After two hours of delving I was totally exhausted. It is going to be impossible to work flat out like this until 26 November. The out-put of sheer energy in terms of the emotions Alceste is going through and the words she speaks is colossal. Even pretending anguish, despair, anger, fear and all the rest is hard enough. But 'pretending' isn't what I understand by the term acting. These emotions, as I am passing through them, are true gut reactions and to be 'in' them totally is using my emotional reserves at the deepest possible level.

We stopped for lunch eventually and they left about 4 p.m. It had been a glorious autumn day, warm enough to have coffee outside and enjoy the marvellous colour of the trees. I hoped to walk later on, but when the house was quiet again all I wanted to do was sleep, which I did, solidly for three hours.

The character becomes nothing less than an obsession. I think about the piece from the moment I wake up and in seven days (is it really only a week?) my basic playing of her has altered quite drastically. It is as if all the study in the world during the past year is not enough. It needs other people, other ideas, the physical feel of the set, and the body going into action on its own account to bring this woman completely alive. We have a long way to go yet, but I can see John is determined to have us 'live' our people as fully as we can from the earliest possible moment. It is a glorious, glorious piece; the nobility of the music and the way Gluck sees the characters through his music is raising us to a high level of inspiration.

Sunday
1 November   Another beautiful warm morning. We raked leaves the colours of a Turkish carpet. It was so peaceful. Evensong at St. Mary's: a gentle, restoring day.

Monday
2 November   Another big day with many people on stage and the correspond-ing slow-down. The chorus were half-jokingly complaining that John expects them to 'emote' genuinely all the time. I thought to myself: Hello, he's been getting at them too! They were exhausted after the morning call.

I turned up in my caftan and low wedge heels instead of trousers tucked into boots, to which I am devoted because they are so warm and comfortable. John wants me to lose my trouser image and concentrate on being feminine and vulnerable. He says I will move and walk differently without my trousers and he could be right. I will try anything. Alceste is already feeling so much softer. We are all affected deeply by the music; nothing about the singing of it is easy.

Tuesday
3 November   After working for one-and-a-half hours with Bob on Act II John suddenly said, 'Come on – let's run it, no stopping.' We sang the scene through. I am always surprised at this moment: the time first elongates; then when we take a run at it the scene miraculously telescopes, and one is spell-bound by the unity and curious as to how so many hours can be spent on such short sections of music. It's rather like stretching an elastic band and

17

suddenly letting it go. Certainly the tension and emotion of a scene is much easier to control when we go through without stopping. At the end of the afternoon when Bob had gone we began my solo scene in Act III, with an entrance down some stairs to Hades. I am frightened of steps because I am short-sighted. It's difficult for me to see the edges and they make me nervous. I did fall once – during *Julius Caesar* after an aria which I sang standing on top of the prompt-box, an exhilarating moment. I turned round, jumped off, and my right knee gave way; I fell quite heavily but my four 'generals' picked me up smartly and carried me off. It is a devastating thing to lose one's balance. The corner I must negotiate on the *Alceste* set will be in semi-darkness and needs a lot of practice in the proper shoes.

Part of the set was put up on Covent Garden stage yesterday morning. Someone who has seen it told me it looked exactly like the music!

Maurits told us a lovely story on the way to tea. It comes from one of the graffiti collections – about the writing on a Yorkshire railway wall which said *Jesus was here*. Someone had written underneath *Only if He remembered to change at Darlington.*

As I left the train at Baker Street to change on to the Circle line I felt a hand on my shoulder, and a perfect stranger said, 'What extraordinary celebrities travel on the Metropolitan line.' He grinned warmly at me and I smiled back. It was so nicely done and I am always just a bit surprised when it happens. Also touched. I usually notice when I'm being stared at even when I'm not wearing my spectacles. The back of my neck goes peculiar. But this man was actually sitting beside me and had avoided making me self-conscious. I was deep in the music of a Strauss song so it was not surprising. I often get some very funny looks as I'm sitting mouthing words to myself. It is absolutely natural to me since I've been doing that on all my journeys for the last quarter of a century. But it must look rather rum. I was sitting beside Keith in the car not long ago waiting for traffic lights to change. A black lady was staring at me in total amazement. I thought, What's up with her? and then realized my mouth had been working away at the score on my lap. From the expression on her face, she obviously thought me a total idiot! I shan't know what has hit me when I no longer need to work on journeys!

Today we had even more bodies at the Opera Centre, the full chorus. We have only had one section of chorus up until now. Everything's slowed down again, so Charles (who came back from Zürich today) Janine and I decided we could use the time to better effect by nipping upstairs to the Green Room and going through some recitatives. Charles, who has lost his voice, announced that at last he really understood what singers feel like with a bad cold. He had been unable to talk to the orchestra during the past two days for longer than half an hour. I thought: Good. Now he knows what we poor devils go through when our equipment packs up. Bob and I have made a pact to take twice our usual amount of extra vitamin C (in effervescent tablet form) and to drag ourselves on for performances even if we are dying! Keeping free of colds is in the lap of the gods, but as Apollo figures decisively in this piece he had better jolly well look after us. The musicians of ancient Greece always asked his blessing; I thing we will too!

Charles is really being his most helpful and constructive self. He solves the problems so easily. In the opening scene of Act I, I have a particularly difficult move and must try to catch his beat and turn many degrees all at the same time. It was bothering me a good deal when he was not there yesterday. But he has completely removed the moment of anxiety by elongating a quaver rest and telling me he will want to bring both the oboe and me in together when he sees me turn. This decision immediately gives me a real sense of both freedom to make the physical move and security to sing the entry.

Later when everybody was together one of the young singers was very firmly reprimanded, quite justifiably; she dissolved in tears, of course, and was unable to sing after that. It is a very hard thing to take, especially when one's colleagues are there, and chorus colleagues – they are watching, and judging all the time. But somehow, the young principals have to face fire, learn to bear it, and come through; it's another of the acid tests of one's worth as a principal. There is always an answer to every problem – as long as one wants to find it. That is also a test – the desire to find a solution, whatever it may do to one's own ideas, in order to give one's best to the piece.

Thursday
5 November 6.30 a.m. I am wide awake and extremely irritated with God for not letting me sleep until 8 a.m. since this is to be a gruelling day and the last thing I need is to start out tired. My annoyance doesn't have the slightest effect except to keep me awake until my breakfast arrives.

9.15 a.m. Dressed, made-up, and in good time for the fast Aldgate train where the film crew is waiting to photograph me

21

handing in my ticket and clambering onto the Covent Garden bus which takes us the final stage of the journey down the Commercial Road to the Opera Centre. There are gremlins on the Metropolitan line and the journey, which lasts a maximum of thirty five minutes at this time of day, takes one hour. I sit there fuming and fretting at the inexplicable delays. It would have to be today!

10.20 a.m. I fall out of the train and Bob Bentley meets me. Charles is also late and we decide to wait for him. He eventually stumbles out of *his* train; he has also been fuming and fretting for similar reasons but we endeavour to calm each other down as we hand in our tickets and climb onto the bus. The production staff waiting in the bus are already fed up with the whole thing and want to go home!

10.30 a.m. We arrive at the L.O.C. and I do a quick explanation on camera as to what the building is and why we are there. The place is the old Roxy Cinema (that's how all the taxi drivers know it) and we are there, heaven help us, because it's the only place we can rehearse in with a floor area equal to Covent Garden stage. There are new rehearsal rooms planned for the Opera House, thank goodness, but of course I shan't ever use them.

10.35 a.m. After a quick coffee, I change into my caftan because it will be a morning on the floor. We are starting with the monologue in Act I when Alceste decides to give up her life for her husband, a deeply emotional and dramatic recitative. We begin. As the camera sweeps across the long line of seated staff, it is highly amusing for me to see them trying hard and unsuccessfully to be natural. I have never seen a more self-conscious collection of people; they are all acting away like mad.

12 a.m. Utterly exhausted and my energy reserves are low. Everyone drinks coffee out of paper cups brought up from the canteen. The sweet canteen ladies are determined to preserve my star status and will not allow me to drink from anything other

than a cup and saucer. There it sits on the top in lone dignity among all the cardboard!

12.18 p.m. Bob and I will go on until 1.30 with the Act II duet scene. When we have done it for the last time there are tears in a number of pairs of eyes and also in mine. I don't know how I shall keep calm when we are playing it for real.

1.30 p.m. I am staggering with fatigue but the film producer, Bob Bentley, needs some more explanatory chat before we break.

1.40 p.m. I have twenty minutes in which to eat a mackerel salad and indulge in a chocolate biscuit. I deserve one.

2 p.m. We go up to the Green Room and I put on my Act I costume. I walk around in it to try out the train which seems inclined to be temperamental.

2.30 p.m. I change into the Act II dress which is half as light again. It needs some adjustment. Gabriella says all materials react differently when they are sewn; she has cut each under-skirt exactly the same but they each behave according to their individual personalities. Keith has arrived with the car. He looks anxious as he sees my face growing whiter with fatigue.

3 p.m. The final dress goes on and as it is pinned I do the last bit of talk for the camera which has taken the entire fitting on film. I signal for a cup of coffee.

3.25 p.m. I change out of the costume and walk down to the car. Keith hands me into it like a piece of brittle glass.

3.29 p.m. We start the journey home.

4.29 p.m. We are still battling through the traffic. London is crazy today, both above and below ground.

5 p.m. I walk into the house like an old, old lady, fill a hot water bottle and climb into bed. I have been drawing upon my energy reserve tanks. This is the feeling which I know perfectly well I can't allow to go on. My emotions have been extended today – emotions heightened by the presence of the camera. In a way, I am 'on show'. Those who sit and direct us, those who sit and listen, cannot even imagine what enormous strength all this effort drains

from us. One of the chorus came up to me yesterday and said, 'I gather this is your last production with us – I want you to know we shall miss you.' I would expect this sort of speech so quietly, simply and sincerely spoken, to fill my heart with a terrible sorrow and regret. But it doesn't, and what I am feeling as I lie here trying to get my strength back for tomorrow is the strongest possible indication that I must not continue to drive myself to the limit. I have never worked beyond my limit but certainly up to it, and would despise myself if I did not. I know so surely that what I have decided is absolutely right.

Rehearsing with John Copley

With Graham Vick (left) and John Copley

Friday
6 *November*   An afternoon of hard and fulfilling work. Felt very jaded after yesterday. Since I was not called until 2 p.m. Keith drove me in. I am using the train for 10.30 calls because the journey would be much longer by car at that hour and apart from being coughed and sneezed at by other commuters there is the added bonus that I needn't get up quite so early.

I stayed in town and joined my friend Julia. Her Cork Street office is my London Club! Many people climb the five flights of stairs, but I, who should have the best pair of lungs, seem to reach the top more out of breath than anyone else! We have a quiet meal in her plant-filled, book-lined office. It is a place where I feel so at home. Her small and devoted staff always make me feel welcome and Julia is the perfect friend. She publishes books and music is her life-blood. I am a professional musician and books are my life-blood. It is the best possible combination. Later as we drive through the quiet Friday streets I realised how long it is since I did anything other than eat, sleep and rehearse.

Sunday
8 *November*   We were clearing leaves again this weekend in ideal conditions, hardly any wind, bright sunshine. Our garden is totally unlike the tiny one we left five years ago. We planted that one entirely ourselves; this one was designed by a Victorian genius, it consists of nothing but large areas of grass, shrubs and magnificent trees; it never looks untidy, probably because of its size. There is always something interesting to look at; in summer a marvellous range of greens, in winter tree sculptures against a background of evergreens. I have never known a garden more responsive to a little care. We have tried to simplify year by year; two acres or thereabouts needs real work but the compensations are myriad.

In the afternoon we all drove into the Opera House; the set was up for a lighting session.

It was strange to see the House on such a day, only technical

26

staff around. They work such long hours making everything possible for us and no-one is around to see. I get the impression that they believe the House really belongs to them, not to us, the performers. I think the House itself is a complete coquette. She was quite prepared to give herself to the production team today, she lets the stage staff believe they own the stage: we have the dressing rooms and that part of the stage in between the dropped curtain and the pit, and the audience is allowed the foyers and the seats. But really, she belongs to herself. It is great to stand on that stage looking out into one of the most beautiful auditoriums in the world. I was very pleasantly surprised to find the sight-lines and the general focus even better than the mock-up set down at the L.O.C. This eases my mind a lot, since the move from the rehearsal room to the stage proper is usually so difficult. My steps, which I tried over and over again, are also an improvement. They are wide with beautiful shallow treads; the set itself is so strongly constructed I can lean my entire weight against it.

Wednesday *11 November* Final day at the L.O.C. and we nearly didn't get there at all; there was a fire in the city during the early hours of the morning which resulted in utter traffic chaos. Everyone eventually arrived and at 10.45 or thereabouts we did a run through of Act I for the first time. Suddenly we were all playing it for real – it was tremendously exciting and exhilarating. By the end of the morning we had been through both Acts I and II. I felt more than ever the sense of being carried along on some great vehicle – Concorde or the Queen Mary, supported by something enormously powerful and of extraordinary quality. I've never known this to such an extent with any other score. It leaves me trembling at the responsibility, carrying the life of the piece in one's hands. I enjoyed so much the actual physical feel of singing the role; everything we have done in the past two and a half

27

weeks is beginning to take shape. This is the last day we shall be together in the relatively intimate space, with all the production and musical staff watching us from a distance of three feet. From now on we are in the theatre itself and I fully expect some unsettling days before we regain the progress made today. I was able to stretch out in my little Green Room, where I had a quiet lunch and recuperated in between the two three hour sessions. I am taking over the character again. My own work is re-asserting itself but my personal authority is immeasurably enriched by everything everyone else has given me. It is so rewarding to see the pleasure in their eyes when a certain thing comes off well.

As I was sitting on the set during a moment's pause some of the stagehands were carrying scenery past me and one of them said out of the corner of his mouth, 'We think you're magnificent!' This remark absolutely made my day!

Thursday
12 *November* The Theatre at last. Now we all feel like a real company once again. Everyone seemed delighted with the set. One of the stage-hands said to me, 'It's nice to put up something that looks like something when you've done it!' I see what he means. The floor space appears to have shrunk but this is because the sides of the set are much closer to us than the walls of the L.O.C. and there is an illusion of less space. We rehearsed with the House lights up; it all looks so beautiful. During these days until the general rehearsal, there is easy communication with the auditorium and the stage because we work with a bridge slung across the pit. It is therefore a simple matter to cross it and go to sit down either to talk over points with Charles or even watch the scene; but as I am on the stage for almost the entire opera I shall see none of the effects when lighting is finalised and costumes appear. John communicates to us from the stalls by microphone, his soft, patient voice filling the House.

28

The projection has changed radically. Instead of a wall ten feet away from us as we have had for the past weeks, we now sing into the open theatre and it is an excellent discipline sending clear mental thoughts to the back of the amphitheatre. It takes much more energy, of course, to do this but even as I am marking the actual voice, I am still throwing the ideas right up there to the farthest seats. I find it fairly easy to keep quite concentrated in fresh surroundings with all that is going on because of my severe short-sightedness; I work in my own space. I shall soon be very much bothered by noise in the flies and the electrics department though, because one can hear instructions being passed to each section loud and clear. Sometimes it's pandemonium up on the stage and the audience never seems to hear any of it, apart from the odd noisy scene change.

My little 'sons' are sweet. I don't know how to reach children or understand how to talk to them. I decided it would be fatal to try by asking them questions or by talking at them. I now find as I am sitting on a step that they will come and sit on either side of me and we have a word or two. They both react very well on stage and I would much rather have two little dears like this than precocious types.

I will spend a lot of time in my dressing room now. At the Garden the number one dressing room is No 5, a strange situation. It is small, incredibly ugly, and the absolute opposite of what anyone would expect. Still, we all hope this will change for the better when the improvements to the back stage area are finished. I took my dressing-table cover in with me today and spread it over the bare wood. This is a piece of rather beautiful material, a copy of a mediaeval tapestry, and it goes with me to every theatre I work in. Just to spread it out there makes me feel that this foreign territory is mine while I am using the room. I often envy the comfortably lived-in look of dressing rooms which belong to actresses during a long run. They really do take on the personality of the occupant. With us, everything personal

Dressing room

must be cleared away after each performance because someone quite different will be using your room the next evening.

And the space shuttle's engine has gone wrong! Poor devils waiting around up there.

Another hard day. We did Act II and it was the ballet dancers' turn to get used to this different space.

The chorus is complaining because of having to kneel down for so long; they are justified; it is a back-breaking, kneeling-down opera – this one. John is trying his best to improve the situation for them.

Keith came in for the tail-end of the rehearsal and saw the final aria; he said to me, 'I only saw that last little bit and I haven't a clue what the scene is about but it was very moving.' It was an interesting reaction from someone who has seen nothing of the piece so far, but straight away it reached him.

We had lunch with Lord Harewood in the room at the rear of the Royal Box. Apparently a German backer wants to make a video recording of *Julius Caesar*; wonderful news but six months too late. How easy it would have been to set this up during the production last spring. How difficult it will be now to find a period when the cast can be reassembled (and in a different theatre) to make a film of an opera I shall not have performed for many months. It is agonising to have to try to find some days which should really be precious rest-times in order that the project can go ahead. I feel such a responsibility to both the cast and our production which was truly special. We are trying for December 1982.

In the afternoon we did some work on Act III in Room 45 over the road. This will be the pattern now, work on stage in the morning and in another room in the afternoon, because the stage staff have to set the theatre for the evening show. It is really hard to work in a small room after being on stage.

31

Our niece Wendy arrived for the weekend this evening. She has had itchy feet for some time and has just found a teaching post in the Philippines – Manila. She goes out there on 2 January and has come to look over all her stuff which is stored in the attic in case there is anything she wants to take with her. She has a lot of courage to strike out on her own so far from home.

Saturday
14 *November*

Our last full day of production. We have now gone through each act on stage. The emphasis will shift yet again when next Monday the music will re-appear from the side-lines and take its rightful place in our attention.

Monday
16 *November*

On this grey, wet, miserable morning, instead of a dreary office I am going into a beautiful Opera House to sing a superb piece of music – what a prospect!

The iron curtain comes down and the principals sit on chairs in front of it, singing, literally over the pit. It is the worst place for us; we feel swamped by the sound coming straight up at us and depressed by the lack of resonance. The band is stroppy and restless; getting on speaking terms with an unfamiliar score makes them irritable. There are a lot of mistakes in the parts and a great deal of valuable time is wasted while the pencils come out and corrections are made. The orchestra plays too loudly all the time because they are still reading from sight and the recitatives sound as though we all have our feet in tins of treacle. Charles has to be a magician, taking note of a thousand things at once, and trying to solve the problems quickly. He is amazing; the way his arms and shoulders communicate and indicate is unbeliev-able. I am surprised to find myself relatively unmoved by the feeling of chaos because I feel the maestro has it all well in hand and I am going to be completely taken care of. I shall sing, and apart from that keep my mouth shut today!

32

John Copley's American protégé (who keeps me supplied with hot chocolate) has been listening to tapes of my 'Charlotte' and 'Mary Stuart' roles. He said in a firm voice as he handed me my first cup, 'Somebody ought to take out an injunction against your retirement from the stage.'

I *do* enjoy singing this score. No; I enjoy the score singing me!

Tuesday
17 November

Saw a man humping bags of cement from a lorry just outside the stage door today. I thought how lucky I was not to have to earn my living like that. He was covered in white dust.

A better morning, the orchestra is settling down and practically no mistakes were discovered during the three hour session. I had a chicken salad brought up to my dressing room at 1.30 p.m. and I sat there with my big outdoor cape and muffler on, freezing with cold (the heating wasn't on), looking at myself and the ghastly room in the dressing-table mirror. I had to bolt down my food and race across the road for a costume fitting before 2 p.m., the time of the afternoon rehearsal. What a glamorous life! I thought. My days begin earlier and earlier. I have to practise thoroughly on orchestral mornings and I stand in my music room dressed for the train trying to put my voice through its paces at 9 a.m. It feels like the middle of the night. As soon as we start make-up, which we do on Thursday, it will be even worse. Members of the chorus keep asking me if I am enjoying singing this role, and of course I reply with an enthusiastic 'Yes.' They would give their eye teeth to be me. I will sing my heart and soul out for them in these peformances and try to make them believe I am worthy of everything which has been poured into my lap for the last twenty-five years. I still think very, very few people would want to bear the staggering burden I shall carry as I wait to go on stage for my first entrance on 26 November. We pay to the last farthing for everything we take from the world. I don't think for a moment that I 'pay' for

33

actually having a voice. That is a free gift to me and I give it back freely. But the outward trappings, fame, a reputation, a 'name', success – these are the things one pays for in other ways, because they *do* come from the world. They are exactly the aspects I shall not miss, it is just these burdens from which I feel such a necessity to free myself and why I have now begun this process. When I am my own person again and have stopped performing altogether, I shall still be a musician. I shall still react to the beauty of music as I have done as long as I can remember. I shall still be a singer because I was born one and I shall die one. But there will be a new joy. My *responsibilities* will be over.

Wednesday I made a friend on the Underground train this morning. A little
18 *November* chap, under two years of age, sitting in his chair, kicking his feet, sucking a dummy, talking to himself, looking at a picture book, pulling his woolly hat over his eyes. Oh! he was having a *lovely* time and when his book got the wrong way up during the hat pulling, he would turn it the right way up when his attention came back to it! I wondered if he was unusual to know which way the right way was – he seemed young to me. His mother was sitting a little distance from him, but he was perfectly happy to be on his own, because *he* couldn't see *her* at all. At one point he dropped his book onto the floor and struggled to lean forward and get it but the strap around his middle prevented this. So I got up and handed it back to him. This was a great event. He eyed me with quiet interest and then directed an unintelligible stream of conversation at me. We exchanged a smile or two, then when I stood up to leave the train he waved me off with his little gloved hand! It was very amusing and very interesting. He wasn't a scrap of bother and well able to amuse himself; altogether the nicest sort of child you could imagine, and a lovely start to my day.

Everything on except make-up at today's rehearsal. We went

over the scenes in Act I, then we went over them again and again. At 1.30, ravenously hungry, I bolted down a bun then changed out of my black and gold Act I costume into my silver white Act II number. Heavenly. It was like changing from chain mail into cotton wool. I went back on the stage for a photographic session with Lord Snowdon; lovely to be photographed by him. He is a real theatre professional, like Zoë, but works in a completely different way from her. I've never seen anyone shoot so fast. I would turn my head through a wide angle, altering the position slightly for each shot and he clicked away at *such* a speed; it was like making a movie, but by hand. Fifty minutes of this and then it was over. He is an exquisitely polite man with beautiful manners; he seemed tense during his work just as I am; well, he's an artist too!

Keith put me into the car and we drove home in appalling traffic and heavy rain. Every bone in my back screamed out in protest against the weight it had supported for three hours. At least during the show, I shall only wear my heaviest costume for about forty minutes or so, nor shall I have to sing all my first act arias more than once. Went to bed immediately and later in the afternoon developed a sort of mild dysentery, a most unusual thing for me. I wondered if the strain of the morning had brought it on.

In Scene II of Act I an enormous, naked male figure, depicting Apollo, stands on the set. When he is not on stage he waits behind in the dark, dominating the whole area. The figure is benign, very beautiful and full of power. I thought in the early stages of production, how significant that we, musicians, play to the god of music.

I think it even more significant now this figure has suddenly appeared. To me he is awe-inspiring and I feel reverence for him. John told me today that in my solo scene at the end of the act the figure appears to be watching over me with kindness, as I make the decision to die for my husband. I am not in the least

35

surprised. The Opera House has a new guest for a little while, someone who really belongs there; the god Apollo; the god of the ancient Greek musicians.

I now have a couch to lie down on in my dressing room.

Friday
20 November
All hell let loose for the past two days! It's like some extraordinary circus; arguments in corridors, people wandering about half in costume, half out. One of the men is wearing a wig which makes him look like Marilyn Monroe, Apollo's chariot is moving in jerks; the male ballet costumes are showing a lot of bum and we are all laughing at the wrong things because we are tired and there is now less than a week to go before first night. Every single problem, major and minor, will be sorted out in time. It's always like this in the later stages. Amid all the chaos something suddenly happens which looks and sounds indescribably beautiful. We are on the right track. When you think of the number of people involved in putting on a single opera it is a miracle. After taking each act for the last three mornings the final phase is a run-through of the complete opera. If we are lucky we may be able to do this on Monday but this is by no means certain. We may only have one chance to go through the piece in the proper order without stopping – that is at the Dress Rehearsal on Tuesday. What a thought! I now have two free days during which I shall talk as little as possible. Talking is positively the worst thing a singer can ever do; talking and catching the common cold.

Monday
23 November
Chaos! Bob Tear pokes his head round the door and says, 'I've got a streaming cold. What shall I do, stay and rehearse or go home?' 'For heaven's sake, go home.' So we have his understudy singing from the side of the stage and one of the production staff, Graham Vick, doing the acting and very well too. After the first

38

act, I simply cannot believe there are two more to go. The film cameras are turning during the last scene of Act I, so I sing out. Earlier on, I just gave full voice in the recitatives and my two little 'sons' got very worried in case this was how I intended doing it on Thursday! After being relieved of my heavy black costume I sat and ate a huge sticky bun, my hunger pangs refusing to be ignored. My little American friend is fully convinced I can't do the job without hot chocolate and keeps bringing me cardboard cups full of it which I duly drink.

As the morning wears on we have to start missing out chunks of Act III and what I feared would happen has. I won't get a run through of the complete opera until the final Dress Rehearsal tomorrow, when an audience of Friends of Covent Garden appear. It is amazing how calmly John Copley behaves. Even more amazing how calmly I behave! My Act III dress hem is still wending its merry way through my legs and threatening to break my neck on the steps; I am trying to tell myself that the pandemonium everywhere is quite natural and right and that all will be well 'on the night'. I come home and get clean and into bed where I shall stay until I rise again tomorrow morning at 7.30 a.m. Thank goodness – only one more early start. My eldest 'son' remarked during the morning, 'You'd think it was the middle of the night in the theatre.' It is always the middle of the night in a theatre because one never sees daylight there; this allied to an early morning feeling, is the last straw; my singer's body knows perfectly well that it is being made to work at the wrong end of the day and is protesting strongly.

Tuesday *24 November* Slap-up breakfast at 7.45 a.m.! I have no difficulty getting up with the rest of the working population, I just hate *doing* it. In my dressing room by 9 a.m. with lots of time to practise and get my face on, but with none to spare. We then ran through the complete opera including the proper intervals and it is a very

39

different matter pacing myself under these circumstances. Gluck has worked things out nicely. There was an audience of Friends of Covent Garden but it is not in any way like a performance and no real sensation of 'people out there' was generated. Nothing is like a performance. The feeling of a complete run was totally tremendous; rather like being on a stupendous horse but having to keep hold of the reins in case he careered off! The emotion in many places really got the better of me, and it was good to have this experience because it will help me not to go 'over the top' on Thursday. Bob's cold is still severe but he sang so well within his capacity, I'm sure he'll be superb. It was a good Dress Rehearsal, better than one could possibly have predicted after yesterday's shambles. But that's the theatre. I can't remember ever looking forward this much to singing anything. It is a glorious role with everything a singer or an actress could ask for.

The weather has turned much colder and the clear morning light over the market was particularly sharp. It seems a hundred years since we began rehearsing *Alceste*; my mind is so completely filled by the score; everything which happened before seems never to have existed, nor does it seem possible that there are other concerts and other pieces of music for me on the farther side of these performances.

Wednesday *25 November* During all these past weeks, packed so tightly with incident, the gathering of ideas, our searching, our works, our laughter, our fatigue, our enjoyment, we have all lived our days with a common purpose. Whatever the result of that purpose may be proved to be when the public sees it tomorrow, nothing and nobody can take away, mutilate, or destroy all that we have learned together and enjoyed during the rehearsal period. It is such a fruitful time in every possible way, and not surprising that I always find these weeks the most enjoyable part of operatic

41

work. They are a microcosm of life, containing a beginning, when we painfully take everything apart, a middle, when we attempt to put it all together again, and an end, our final Dress Rehearsal, which is a death. A death, because the preparation is ended and something totally new begins; rehearsals are very far removed from the real performances. There is an enormous gulf between the two and no bridge. One thing finishes completely and the new moment starts. The performances too will have a life – a beginning, a middle and an end, and that process will be full of its own interesting events.

Today, then, is a sort of sadness because the camaraderie is over. I won't see much of people in general because I shall be either shut away in my dressing room or out on the stage working and then home to hibernate until the next appearance. If I have learned anything from these rehearsals it would probably be a heightened sense of detachment; having a deep interest in, and concern for, all the experiments going on around me but able to stand in a fairly calm sort of centre, firm in the knowledge that all would eventually be well – except for the very first day which I am sure was the result of physical fragility – my migraine the day before. I do feel so utterly grateful for the knowledge of other people – the staff who have literally poured their expertise into me in order to help me create this role. I believe I emerge from this process each time a better performer. People in my profession, who are really good, and really interested in the music first and foremost, are always totally generous with what they know. All knowledge has one over-riding desire to be passed on and used. It is a humbling thing to be at the receiving end of so much given so unstintingly, and with what feels like affection.

Thursday
26 November The day I have been working towards for over a year. How do I feel? Well rested, raring to go. No butterflies in the solar plexus at all. Maybe they will start later. (They do not.) I have my

breakfast, open a fistful of loving wishes from family and closest friends, then wash my hair which will look absolutely awful at the party, after being flattened under my wig all night long. At mid-day I open the piano and start to practise, the voice seems to be in good shape. A light lunch and back to bed. I still feel exhilarated and am looking forward tremendously to curtain-up. I sleep for about an hour, but I must lie and rest until 4.15 when Keith brings me my dinner! This consists of steak and salad and a glass of milk. I have packed away my entire ration of calories for the day by mid-afternoon so that should be enough energy to last me through the performance.

We are out of the house by 5 p.m. and I am at the stage door by 5.50, to pick up a bundle of mail and a warm kiss from the door-man which pleases me very much. The heating is off in my dressing room! I look at all my telegrams and cards, put my cloth on the dressing-table, clean my face thoroughly and begin to make-up. I am absolutely calm, proved by the steadiness of my hand as I draw lines above my eyes with a fine paint brush. I practise at intervals and the pace quickens as the half hour is called, people come in constantly, my 'sons' arrive in the next door dressing room. They squeal with laughter and excitement, a lovely sound coming through the wall. I like to be ready in good time and have left two hours for preparation today. I need all of that because when the five minute call is given I am only just be-wigged and costumed.

Bob Tear is ill; his cold has settled on his chest but he is going to try and sing. I spend the last few moments pacing my dressing room and then make my way back stage passing the statue of Apollo as I do so. I greet him silently for a few moments and then wait for my cue. I feel calm and strong and full of joy to have such a role in such a House, and then walk out onto the stage. This first moment is unlike any of the rehearsal entrances. Now the final piece of the jig-saw puzzle is in place – the vital ingredient of all performances, the audience. With our weeks of work, our

43

strivings and struggles towards some sort of perfection, we are helpless until the people are there to complete the circle; no magic, no communication, is possible until this moment, it is all self-indulgence until now. This living wall of human feeling reaches out to me across the pit and locks into my heart; the performance can unfold. The first act goes by like a flash and I go back to my dressing room knowing that I have sung that glorious music with my whole heart and soul.

I change into my Act II costume and the wig is redressed. I have perhaps five minutes flat on my back on the couch before I go out again. Bob is in great difficulty and in anguish. I feel equal anguish for him, knowing how we have worked towards this moment, and what we have achieved in rehearsal. We reach the end of the act and I have another short rest before Act III. Bob has deteriorated and cannot speak, never mind sing! He is going to act with me, but his understudy is to sing the role from the pit. It is difficult for me to hold my concentration in my character, when the sound I am working with emerges from a different place; I am making super-human efforts to try to compensate for the strange discrepancy between the action on stage and the sounds coming from the pit. The curtain comes down on Act III and it is over.

We have all tried so terribly hard to carry on naturally and to an extent I think we have succeeded. The curtain parts time and again as we take our applause, then suddenly the stage is crowded with people, management, staff, friends, all mixed up with cast. The film cameras are busy recording the moment and follow me right back to the dressing room. More people, masses of flowers, it is pandemonium, everyone squeezing into spare corners, there is so little room, people ask me how I feel. I say something; eventually everyone goes and I climb out of my costume. The wig I have worn for three and a half hours is removed. I wash and change, trying to get into the party mood because we are going to the Garrick Club for dinner. As I sit restoring my appearance to

44

normal I realize I am stunned. I have used up so much emotion and energy during the evening, there is absolutely nothing left. I go down to the stage door and sign autographs while Keith fills the boot of the car with flowers.

The cameras are awaiting our arrival at the Garrick to film some of the proceedings and Lord Gibson's speech after dinner. I am talking quite normally to my neighbours, Charles on one side and John Tooley, the General Director of Covent Garden, on the other. All the time I am thinking: What am I doing here? Part of me is functioning and part of me aches for peace and quiet and the opportunity to recover slowly from the evening. We are home at 2 a.m. and I am asleep before I know it.

The things I shall remember from this day are strangely diverse. We heard during the morning that the son of a friend of ours had been murdered. A terrible, shocking event; we felt dreadful for the parents and couldn't get the news out of our minds. Keith didn't want to tell me but I'm glad he did. The everyday world marches side by side with the one in which I am understandably immersed – the raw, cruel, painful fact of murder exists right alongside the fact of our make-believe and our music. This is how it is; somehow we have to live with the horrifying contradiction. Then there was the unusual calm confidence of my feelings about the performance. Every time I was conscious that today was 'the day', instead of the sickening lurch of terror in the mid-riff I felt nothing except eagerness and joy to be singing a great role. My physical inadequacies had decided to opt out and allow me to perform with maximum control, to me this was nothing else but a miracle. Lastly there was Bob's illness. After all our hard work, the work of many, many people, our performance was at the mercy of the common cold. I felt such anger about this and total helplessness as well. Grief-stricken for Bob too. It could so easily have been me! But however hard we work, however well we prepare, human beings cannot create perfection. It is right to try, wrong to feel

46

disappointed when we fail. Perfection is not the human condition. I must be content to know that I believe I sang this magnificent role as well as I am able, without having to battle against fear. For this reason alone I can claim this night as one of the most remarkable of my whole career, perhaps the *most* remarkable, as an experience of enormous joy.

Saturday   I love the story told by a friend of the great naturalist painter,
28 November   Tunnicliffe, who, at the age of 78, with failing eyesight and after a working life of enormous output, one day laid aside his pens and brushes and said, 'Ah've dun me whack.' Exactly!

Alceste, Act II

Alceste, Act II

A second performance that was like a first night. And of course literally, it *was* our first night, with Bob in great form and all systems go. Already our performance has begun to change and to grow; as a living whole, it should do. We make the same moves and sing the same notes but there is a difference and that will be true of each one. The attention and stillness of the audience was remarkable tonight, at least until the amount of dry ice floating out into the theatre in Act III made people cough! I think the technical boys let their hands slip a bit.

Julie Andrews told me later over dinner about the amazing performance Lena Horne is giving on Broadway, at the age of sixty-five. It is obviously not to be missed when we are in New York in January. It sounds a truly remarkable feat and I cannot

50

imagine how anyone finds the strength at such an age to go through six shows a week plus two matinees.

It is a clear, sharp morning, quite still, a beautiful day. I am sitting here absolutely drained of energy and emotion; suddenly the sun shines through my music-room window as if determined to do its best to replace my strength in the next forty-eight hours before I go through it all again. These tremendous heights and depths have been the pattern of my life; I suppose what attracts me so much to what I call a 'normal' life is the hope that my later years may be spent on a more even keel and that a measure of outward peace will help me to achieve an inward one. If I could develop the same quietude in the midst of work, that would indeed be a victory. The chemical circumstances of adrenalin flow probably make this impossible.

I saw the suggested design of my book this morning, an indescribable delight. I almost believe there will actually BE a book next year when I see pages of lay-out spread in front of me. To create something entirely from scratch is to me, a recreator of other people's work, the most satisfying feeling in the whole world.

I do not pretend there is anything the least original in my experiences, but putting them down on paper is a new feeling for me. My strongly held belief that we are all totally individual and therefore see our lives in unique ways, justifies writing down my own.

Friday
4 December
'Ladies of the chorus, please do not go on stage wearing jewellery and nail polish. Gentlemen, SOCKS OFF! At the last performance red and blue ones were to be seen. Please wear the socks provided.' I looked at Rose (my dresser) in amazement, as Stella, our stage manager, made this statement over the tannoy just before the show.

51

Apparently some of the girls are reluctant to be parted from their favourite things and go on stage wearing an extraordinary conglomeration which doesn't fit in with their costume at all! And the boys won't change their socks! I hastily checked to see if I had removed *my* nail polish.

Our third performance and the usual pattern is not in evidence. In every production I've known there is a tendency for opening night to be a tremendous 'high', the second a corresponding 'low', and the most dangerous moment of the run because everyone is reacting from the excitement and concentration goes. The later ones gradually pull away from this level to something stable, good, and of a fairly general standard. Not so with *Alceste*. Our low point was first night as a result of illness. The second was like a first night and the third performance even better; most unusual and unique in my experience. The role is certainly the most taxing, vocally and physically, that I've ever done. I leave my dressing room at the beginning of each act and don't set foot in it again until the end of the act. I get tired but the exhilaration and enjoyment seem to carry me through; I am beginning to feel increasingly free within the framework of the production, and new aspects of emotion reveal themselves. I've never enjoyed anything more than this piece.

Saturday *5 December* If someone asked if my career has been 'worth it', in other words worth the sacrifices made by me and members of my family, worth the separations, the agony of performing, of trying to keep perfectly fit, the undying battle against nerves, the strains and pitfalls of being a public figure, my honest answer would have to be 'No'.

This sounds a terrible comment to make on a career which, in terms of the world, has been a highly successful one. I have done everything any singer could dream of, yet the moments when the musical rewards have equalled the price one has to pay for them have been few.

But if someone were to ask me how I would choose to be born in order to learn about life, I would unquestionably reply, 'As an artist.' If it is, as many people suggest, a rather special privilege to be born one, the privilege lies in the opportunities such an existence provides for the individual to learn about himself; in the questions artistic life forces one to ask and try to answer; in the struggle to come to terms with performing and everything implied by an act of heroism, which demands the baring of the soul before strangers, and public judgement of this act; in the choices to be made as a result of loving something more than oneself and serving that something with the greatest integrity one is capable of. Yes, in these terms, my career *has* been 'worth it', a thousand times over. I am lucky to be born with one outstanding talent; it makes the direction of my life clearer; but I do sincerely believe that every human being is an 'artist' in the sense that everyone can make of his life a 'work of art', it all depends on the way we look at so-called 'ordinary' things. The ideal of Zen Buddhism is to make every single action a perfect meditation and this is exactly what I mean.

It has always intrigued me in the Parable of the Talents that the man with ten (the greatly gifted) and the man with five (the gifted in a diverse way) end up with *exactly* the same reward. The man with one talent would have received just what the other two did if he hadn't been such a clot.

Whatever our ambitions are, they surely all add up to the desire for happiness and fulfilment. It may even be easier to have both these qualities living the life of an 'ordinary' person because success has its own problems; but regardless of the responsibility caused by a gift, in my case, a voice, I thank God on my bended knees that I *am* an artist. And that *Alceste* is worth every penny of the price I am paying for it!

53

Sunday
6 December
Our front drive-way is made of York stone and lethal when wet. Keith decided to give the surface a thorough going-over today with a chemical scourer to peel off fungus and make it safer; he got out there early with my father and Uncle Phil who, together with his wife Hilda, had been to Friday's performance and stayed here with us. The three men got stuck in with brushes and made short work of the job. Hilda meanwhile got stuck in with the tape and measured me in all the usual places and in some very unusual ones for my Glyndebourne wardrobe form. As I jotted down the numbers it made depressing reading. For a singer I am definitely on the small side. For a fashion-conscious female I am definitely *not*!

Phil and Hilda are Keith's uncle and aunt on his mother's side. I imagine many people have reason to be grateful to them, because their acts of kindness, generosity, and neighbourliness are myriad, but I reckon I come extremely high on the list. As they live in Wendover, not too far from us, we see them often and my parents would always stay with them for a time when we were away for long periods abroad. It was a great comfort to know they were together.

In January 1977 Keith and I were in New York and had just booked into our hotel. We went into lunch and began opening a large pile of mail; among the letters was a cable from a friend – a neighbour of ours. It informed me that my mother had suffered a stroke the night before; her condition was stable. Time does some strange things at moments like these. I watched people eating their food; I looked at passers-by in the street, and couldn't understand why no-one seemed to notice my agony. I felt as though my body had screwed itself up into a taut ball and deposited itself in my solar plexus, a dense incredibly hard lump.

Somehow we got upstairs and phoned my father. He had been wakened in the night by my mother sitting bolt upright, but unable to speak. He understood what had happened, went to the telephone immediately, and called an emergency service. When

54

the doctor arrived he confirmed a stroke but did not propose to take her into hospital, although both her speech and movement were affected. Out of my mind with anxiety I said, 'But Daddy, how are you going to manage on your own?' He replied, 'Don't worry. I've called Phil and Hilda who were due here for the weekend and as soon as Hilda heard the news she said they would be over in two hours. She sent a message to tell you they will both stay here with us until you get back.' I felt a tremendous sense of relief at his words, knowing that these two were the ideal people in such an emergency. I then called the doctor myself and was advised not to return because my mother would immediately have believed her condition to be more serious than it was. I came away from the telephone shattered by the knowledge that she was lying there unable to communicate, and I was three thousand miles away.

The stroke could certainly have been more serious. On the other hand my mother could have had another one at any time, and my dilemma was cruel beyond belief. Every fibre of my being ached with worry for her; I longed to get on the plane and return to London. I gave my Carnegie Hall recital and another one in Toronto with so much inner pain, that even now I simply cannot believe it was possible to sing under such emotional stress. There was also extreme resentment in my heart: I kept thinking: What am I doing here singing to all these strangers? I want to be at home. Work doesn't matter under these conditions. I want to be at home. But I stayed and I sang and every moment I was waiting for the phone to ring and to hear that I was too late to see her alive. I cannot even now decide whether I was right or wrong to allow my sense of duty to my profession to over-ride my deepest personal longing. If she had gone from me at that time I would never have forgiven myself, and I would have been left with a deep and lasting resentment towards my job. But fate decided otherwise. I finished my tour and I returned to London and early one morning I held her in my arms and looked at the little twisted face and heard the

55

gallant attempts to speak. Funnily enough, I always understood what she was trying to say.

The months went by and she became almost normal. Exactly a year later, I was right there beside her during the final weeks of her life; by a strange coincidence my American tour had been planned for the spring and for the first time in many years I was at home during the month of January. I took her in and out of hospital, I was in the house when she went into a coma, and we buried her with my brother in York, the resting place she had always wanted. I don't know what kind of guardian angel arranged all this but I have a feeling that by remaining in New York the year before, I was given a chance a year later to be at her side when she needed me most.

Now, four years later, I looked down at Hilda busy measuring me and thought as I think each time I see her, that somehow the world pays back to people what they give out; there are no two people more deeply loved than she and Phil, no two people who deserve it more.

Monday
7 December
I read a piece in *The Times* which stated that the higher a voice sings the less intelligible words will be. This is absolutely true; the poor high soprano has the devil's own job to project consonants; beautiful tone for her must take precedence over clear diction. I've always felt lucky to be a mezzo; not only is the repertoire varied and interesting but most of the time lies at a tessitura where words *can* be intelligible. Sound has a tremendous effect, but allied to words its ability to move and stir the emotions is colossal. I could never have been an instrumentalist; sound alone is not enough for me, as a performer.

Words have fascinated me as far back as I can remember. I was about four and a half when I learned to read and the moment when the marks on paper made sense to me was a revelatory one,

56

full of wonder and joy. My respect for words, spoken and sung, has been total because I know how far-reaching their power can be.

I learned to talk before I was two and at about two and a half was greatly influenced by a gang of workmen building a house on a site next door to us. This influence continued for some months and I visited the men every day, teddy tucked underneath my arm, to make sure they were getting on alright. It ceased rather abruptly one morning when, work halted by a late delivery, my mother found me unexpectedly in our garden and asked me why I wasn't helping the builders. I calmly looked up at her and replied, 'We're buggered for bricks!'

Tuesday
8 December
We woke to find our garden had turned white overnight. It was a glorious sight, silver as far as the eye could see, thanks to the brilliant Victorian landscape gardener who planned our modest two acres to look like a park. To us it is the most beautiful view in the world especially when we are thousands of miles away from it. No trains are running, the road outside the house is in a dreadful state and we have a most important luncheon date at the Garrick Club where a small group of Emmie Tillett's closest friends is meeting to celebrate her eighty-fifth birthday.

Dear Emmie has been my agent all my working life until a stroke (from which she fully recovered) made her decide, at over eighty, to call it a day. She is of the old school; a great lady, a tough business woman with high standards which she expects all her artists to uphold. She first heard me sing at the Lotte Lehmann Master Classes in the Wigmore Hall in 1956, and was on the telephone to me immediately. To be taken up by Ibbs and Tillett was the best possible start to a singing career. As the years passed I came through the ranks working with each department head, until the day finally came when Emmie and her assistant Beryl

57

Ball dealt with my engagements personally. Now Beryl looks after me on her own.

Emmie and I made history together when, in January 1967, we both went to New York for my first Carnegie Hall recital. I had been a success the previous November, doing a number of concerts in New York, so Sol Hurok, my American agent, decided to put on this recital very quickly in order to launch me, as he put it, 'into the big time'! The Hurok office and the Tillett office were on the most friendly terms and Sol and Emmie knew each other well. For many years Sol had tried his best to persuade Emmie to cross the Atlantic and pay him a visit but she couldn't see much point in leaving England. As we walked into Sol's office the place went wild, because no-one knew that Emmie Tillett herself had decided to come with me. Sol Hurok's face was an absolute picture and Emmie, of course, was delighted to think that her surprise visit had caused exactly the furore of excitement she had intended. I was thrilled and honoured by her decision to come with me; she was echoing a situation of some years previously when her beloved husband, John Tillett, had crossed the Atlantic with the equally beloved Kathleen Ferrier. Our journey was a pilgrimage to honour theirs. Emmie often spoke about our visit afterwards and decided that four days was the perfect length of time to stay away from London! Her artist, on the other hand, has toured the U.S.A. North, South, East and West, every single year since! And loved it!

So today, there we were in a small room, drinking our friend's health, showing her by our presence round the table something of the devotion we feel for what she is and what she stands for. To me, the attitude she has revealed at times when I have had to cancel because of illness has been a thing for which I never cease to thank her. There have not been many such moments in a long career, but it is truly dreadful knowing one is going to let the public down and the understanding of one's agent is essential. Emmie has never once failed me in this. Quite

58

apart from an agent with all that implies in terms of mutual trust and confidence, she has been a friend and I owe to her and to Beryl an immense debt.

Wednesday
9 *December*
Still completely ice-bound. We walked over the hill during the morning to get some much needed exercise, revelling in the sparkling light and invigorating air, and called in at our local shop for some bread. The young man behind the counter was singing 'I'm dreaming of a white Christmas' at the top of his voice, pausing only to assure us that summer was just five months away!

Practised before lunch then a long but sleepless rest and into the theatre by six. For the first time Keith noticed empty seats, not surprising in the conditions at the moment. They must all have been paid for though; since the Dress Rehearsal we have been trying to pull strings for various frantic friends who couldn't buy a ticket for love or money; the only possibility is returns on the day or queuing for the amphitheatre.

There were eight members of the chorus absent because of illness; there is something going around; only two more performances to go and I do so want to be fit.

Once again we progress, dramatically and musically. Since last Friday we have changed, all of us, as human beings and therefore as performers. The differences may be small and unnoticed by anyone but ourselves, but they are there. The Universe changes at every moment of existence, and it must follow that human beings do too.

It is useless for me to try and 'do' anything myself to make each performance fresh; it is fatal to get out there and 'try'. The harder one does this, the less effective the end result is. But there is a sort of trick in relying on ability and technique, letting the rest 'be done' through the medium of the body and personality. The more successful this process is, the less the performance is

59

'mine'. If anything of value is achieved it is certainly NOT 'mine', neither is responsibility for so-called failure. In these circumstances there is no failure because I have no control whatsoever over the power which touches another human being. If such power is to work at all, half the responsibility lies with the person at the receiving end. This implies an equally great humility, from both artist and audience. They must both be empty of self and receptive. The performer has to stand aside and allow himself to be used. The listener should come with an open heart and mind, a certain generosity of spirit, putting aside the worries of the day, the memories of other performances, and ready to absorb the present moment. Music has the power to enrich us if we allow it to do so, but only when the circumstances are right.

Friday Weather conditions worse but it is a gloriously sunny day. Joan
11 *December* and Geoff, Keith's sister and her husband, are due for the weekend
to see the opera and the prospect for any sort of travel seems bleak.
Christmas itself will be bleak for the families of the school boys
who died in the train crash outside Beaconsfield today. What utter
desolation for the parents.

My first experience of death was at ten years of age when I
stood by my brother's bed-side and watched him die. Six o'clock
on Sunday evening, 5 March 1944.

Peter, four years older than I was, had been born with a weak
heart valve aggravated by an attack of scarlet fever. Always a
delicate boy, his health gradually became more precarious and my
parents, having watched over him as an invalid practically all his
life, finally had to watch him slip away from them. I had grown
used to seeing him either in bed or in a wheel chair, hardly able,
even when he was on his feet and going to school for a brief period,
to play cricket or be an ordinary boy. In some ways he was a
decidedly extraordinary boy; he possessed a most beautiful

61

singing voice; he was incredibly handsome with fine bone structure and piercing blue eyes. His fragility made him look like an absolute thoroughbred and indeed his was an extremely refined gentle spirit. In total contrast I looked like a sturdy little pit pony with a nature to match. But apart from the usual brother and sister scraps (he thoroughly disapproved of my swearing) we loved each other deeply.

Now I knew I was about to say 'goodbye' to my brother; my grandparents had arrived and we went straight up to Peter's room. He was lying calm and quiet and smiled as we entered; the evening light fell onto his bed; my mother took him in her arms. He remained with his head on her breast, then suddenly sighed deeply. It was all so quick, so peaceful, so *natural*. I could not understand what had happened but my mother took me downstairs; as she did so, the smell of death unlike any other smell in the world filled the house – sickly, sweet.

In the months and years which followed, we were a family of three but felt like a family of four, always something missing; I remember the heart-rending sight of my mother as I came in from school, bending over her baking, tears running into the pastry. We were all scarred each in our different ways. It is a terrible thing to lose a child. The grief in our house was like a mountain pressing down upon me. What this death did to me I shall never know. It certainly did something. I became ill some months later, suffering from delayed shock. Eventually we moved away and went to live in another town altogether but my parents never got over losing their son. They were 'wounded' people. I have never felt like an only child because I remember, if somewhat cloudily, the days when I had a brother.

I know what the parents of these small boys are going through at this present moment; snow, ice, a howling wind blowing, and Christmas, the feast of children, looming up ahead; for these families Christmas will never be the same again.

Joan and Geoff can't get down tonight. They will try the train tomorrow.

They arrive, poor things hours and hours late, but full of good humour. What a wonderful attitude after such a journey. They have time to snatch a meal, change, and we are off to the theatre. Surely we won't have an audience tonight – the conditions are appalling? I go up to my dressing room to find it is my birthday – for there stands an enormous basket of fruit, which is a present from Ron Freeman (wigs) and Elaine. My birthday is really in August, and there isn't a good reason why they should have done such a lovely thing.

I make a complete hash of my make-up, the eyes just will not go right so have to clean it all off and start again. As I am finishing and still none too pleased with the result, in comes a huge iced cake with candles, and an inscription 'La voix eternelle' done in a highly professional way by a very kind male fan. A real work of art. It *must* be my birthday! Tonight's performance is broadcast and the house is again packed out. Afterwards, many of the staff come round to say it is the best yet. My dressing room is crammed with family; we are joined by our nephew and his wife and her mother. It is a particular pleasure when I know people are out there who are special to me. My sister-in-law, who has seen everything I've done and who is a most sensitive and deeply feeling person, tells me this role is my finest. She is deeply disappointed to be seeing only one performance and had got a great deal out of this evening; since she teaches French, her grasp of the libretto and its nuances is particularly strong. Her understanding and unfailing support for over twenty-five years is precious to me.

63

I suppose I died a little tonight.

This extraordinary run has grown richer all the time and our final performance was a culminating peak, true to the pattern established by the others.

As I look back over the weeks since that first morning, the entire period has overflowed with amazing experiences; interchange between people, exchange of ideas, of knowledge and a steady increase in our command over the special idiom Gluck demands, inspired by the sheer quality of the score.

At the final moment, after we had played to an audience generating unbelievable excitement and good-will, the whole place erupted and Sir John Tooley came out onto stage to speak. My heart sank; I thought he might say something to the company behind a decently dropped curtain but it hadn't crossed my mind that the audience would be included as well. He said wonderful things but his over-riding emotion was one of gladness for me. I could not have wished for a more understanding grasp of my situation. How much better to make my farewell in these circumstances than to peter out like a spent candle. To choose the circumstances of one's going is a privilege; in my case, there is not the slightest tinge of regret; sadness at parting with friends and colleagues but regret – no.

After Sir John had spoken he presented me with a set of rare prints, representing Gluck operatic characters, a real treasure, and I stepped forward to say 'Thank you'. My courage failed me completely! The moment was just too much for me; I tried to say the words which were in my heart but I doubt if many people actually heard them. What I attempted to explain was my feeling that all I had to say I had already said and in the best possible way by my performance on stage that night. I was told by many people later that the tears in my eyes were shared by many in the House. We took more curtain calls and on my final one the audience rose to its feet. I've had standing ovations before, but never one like this. Usually the audience rises in sections but this

64

Making-up for the final performance

With Sir John Tooley (right) and Sir Charles Mackerras after the presentation at the end of the last Alceste performance

one literally 'rose like one man', just as the expression describes; it was absolutely amazing.

Flowers and more flowers, in my arms, at my feet, and thrown from above, then curtain down for good and more 'good-byes' both back-stage and in my dressing room.

It took a long time to change but eventually I packed my dressing-table cloth into my theatre bag, took a last look at the funny, drab little room and made for the stage door, where there were more crowds, more flash photographs, more autographs to sign.

Finally everything was completed and we drove away to L'Opera where we were meeting five dear friends, the only people we wanted to be with on such a night. Supper was an hilarious affair but with much serious talk as well, the perfect combination. The kind people from a neighbouring table who insisted on sending over champagne and who had been at the performance, must have been amused to see our enjoyment.

At last time to go home and bed by 2 a.m. after one of the greatest nights of my life, a memory to cherish, always.

Just before Stella, the Stage Manager, pushed me out for my final curtain-call she said to me, 'Come on, we've switched on every light in the place for you.' Out I went and gazed at the House in all its glory, ablaze with light, colour, cheering people, flowers, and for one brief, wonderful moment, just for me!

At the stage door after the last night

Part Two

American Tour, January 1982

A wonderfully happy family Christmas, perhaps the best ever, is over. Relatives have departed, the tree has been undressed and put out for the dustmen, my niece has flown far away to the Philippines, and I have hugged my father, whom I now leave for some weeks in order to tour the U.S.A. Keith and I have made this journey every year since 1966, when I first went to San Francisco. I usually dream about flying very low over the water during the night before we go, but not this year. The preparations for the trip seem to have gone especially smoothly and my mind is calm, my heart unworried, as I sit in a plane bound for Minneapolis surrounded by children – an un-accompanied one next to me – card players – talkers – sleepers and cabin staff. I certainly feel much less like a herded animal than usual because we left for the first time from Gatwick, a quieter airport than Heathrow – at least it was today. At long, long last, I suppose I am learning that whatever measure of stability, peace and contentment is to be had must come from inside, and is carried around with us wherever we happen to be. From the moment we leave home the petty irritations begin; every simple thing we want for the next month we must ask someone else to get or do for us. We find that three weeks is just about the maximum time to elapse before we reach screaming point.

The tour is very well planned and all the concerts are recitals. This makes things so much easier because I have only two different recital programmes to carry in my head, and although we have a good deal of travelling to do at least a free day is just that, and not a day when I am called to rehearse with an orchestra. As we did quite a lot of work together in London last week, my accompanist Martin (Isepp) need not join us until

71

Friday. Because I suffer severely from jet lag, I travel well ahead in order to get my body in good shape before I sing on Sunday.

Touring puts a big burden on Keith who, together with the Shaw office in New York, has planned this tour down to the last detail and now has two musicians to look after, to book in and out of airports, hotels and concert halls, ensuring that we are always at the right place at the right time. Apart from the actual concerts, Martin and I can bask in the luxury of such treatment and let him get on with it. He is very good at his job. I never cease to bless my luck in finding a man who takes all the practical burdens from my shoulders, leaving me free to sing, and who remains at the same time a strongly individual, completely independent person. He does his job, I do mine, and it is a wonderful partnership. About two years ago an extraordinary rumour went around the profession that our marriage was on the rocks. Where it came from, how it arose, we never knew. It caused us great amusement. I have, however, made Keith promise that if ever it did happen he would come back each week to do my books, organise the income tax, and calculate the V.A.T.!

A career like mine is nothing more nor less than a business which has to be run strictly. Keith calls me the Chairman of the Board; he is the Managing Director and says that all decisions are, finally, mine. In this he is perfectly correct, but the Chairman could not function without the Managing Director's unending resources of commonsense, patience, and Northern firmness. I feel great compassion for those of my colleagues who travel around the world *sans* spouse, children and sanity. It is a lonely life. A very small proportion of the time is spent in actual performance. Think of all the hours to be 'filled in' just living, and all the people one wants to be with thousands of miles away. You have to love your work, or rather be obsessed by it, in order to survive.

72

Working with Keith

Minneapolis,
Thursday
7 January I was awakened by Niagara Falls thundering through the bedroom; it was our next door neighbour taking his 6 a.m. bath. All hotels, without exception, seem to have intertwined plumbing, forcing the occupants to share each other's habits at all times of day or night. The only quiet bedroom I know is my own at home, and I might just as well bow to the inevitable and realise that I will not have a peaceful or unbroken night's sleep until I get back to it.

The saving grace of Minneapolis in this impossible cold is the sky-walk system which connects many of the big department stores in such a way as to enable one to walk under cover for practically the whole length of the main street. We tried the open air but soon gave in. The cold attacks so savagely that one's skin feels as though it's coming away from the face. Today we

73

suddenly heard the sound of a piano being played and gravitated, fascinated, towards it. There in a huge brick-walled atrium was a young pianist seated at a small boudoir grand, playing Rachmaninoff; his audience was engaged in a number of different activities, eating lunch from paper-bags, reading newspapers, quietly talking, even listening! It was an excellent test for the young man's concentration and he was making decent music from a poor instrument. There were trees in pots, flowers in tubs, masses of people riding up and down a moving staircase – and it could only happen in America. We sat and listened. Martin arrived later this evening looking as fresh as a daisy after his gruelling flight from London. Now the team is complete and we will start work tomorrow.

Martin's mother was my singing teacher for many years until she died. I studied French and English repertoire for a time with Meriel St. Clair, who helped me greatly in this area; Helena Isepp gave me my technique and introduced me to the vast world of the German *lied*. Martin was an Army officer in 1953 doing his National Service when I first met him; as the years passed he began to play for me both in the concert hall and in my early recordings. He is one of the most deeply sensitive musicians I have ever met and his qualities as a gentle, kind, and understanding person inevitably spill over into his music. I do not know of anyone in our profession who is regarded with more affection, which approaches adoration where his students are concerned. He discovered quite early on in his career a real ability for teaching, which began at Glyndebourne, continued at Juilliard in New York, and now has brought him back to England as head of music both at the wonderful National Opera Studio recently started in London and at Glyndebourne as well. These two threads, performing as accompanist and as teacher, run through his life together and exploit to the full his outstanding musical and human qualities. His wife Rose is a marvellous support, a source of strength and commonsense, and

74

he has two splendid sons, Matthew and Peter, who sometimes play cricket on our lawn, but not nearly often enough. He misses his family terribly on tour and we do our best to cheer him up, but 'there is no substitute for wool'!

Friday
8 January Rehearsed at the hall during the afternoon, a modern university building with a seating capacity of eighteen hundred. Just the right size. As we drove there, we crossed a Mississippi very nearly frozen over. Hundreds of miles away to the south lies New Orleans enjoying temperatures far removed from ours. Students like to get into small boats and journey all the way down there for fun. What a wonderful way to see the country.

During rehearsal, I noticed how much my breath control is affected by jet lag, but with another forty-eight hours to go before the concert I should be alright. Returned to the hotel and did a TV interview, which left no time for a rest before we went to dinner with the Argentos, Dominic and Carolyn. Dominic is the resident composer at the University of Minneapolis. He wrote a major work for me a few years ago – a song cycle, set to words he had taken from the diary of Virginia Woolf, which won a Pulitzer Prize. We spent a happy evening with them, eating Carolyn's beautiful food which she served with the greatest care on exquisite china; they have collected a great deal during their yearly trips to Europe, and since they spend three months in Florence their home has an Italian flavour. Being in that house, eating home-cooked food surrounded by lovely things, made us feel like Bedouins reaching an oasis, even after only three days.

Keith leaped out of bed in the early hours, furious with the people next door who were creating merry hell about something. After hammering violently on the wall with his shoe, silence fell. Six a.m. and up he got again, this time to remonstrate very politely with people on the *other* side, who were having an extremely loud conversation. Surprised to find they were

75

disturbing us, they too became quiet and we tried to go off to sleep again.

What do people think of when they come to hotels? Incidents like these are commonplace, an undisturbed night a rarity. Radios and television are switched on loudly, regardless of the time of night. Guests make no attempt to talk softly as they walk along corridors. The maids clatter cups and saucers and shout to each other from an early hour. We stay in beautiful hotels – and we might as well pitch a tent in the middle of the street for all the peace we get. We try to see the funny side of it, but the only thing which makes us laugh is Keith's face when he returns from his sorties: he leaves the room in fury and returns moments later with a sheepish grin on his face saying, 'They were very nice about it really.'

The noisy people next door are part of a Canadian ladies' conference. Last night they decided to have a party and at 2.30 a.m. they were raising hell. Having pinched everyone's DO NOT DISTURB notices from the doors, they proceeded to set the fire alarm off 'by accident'. There were so many people in the room, smoking, that the sensitive alarm system read a fire warning from the air pollution! It was frightening to hear the alarm go, especially since conditions were too cold for us to wait outside until the fire engines came. But it was a false alarm, the management disbanded the party next door, and we all tried to sleep again. Some time later little fingers tap-tapped at our door, and when Keith answered it, there stood a group of ladies asking if this was the party? 'No, it isn't,' Keith thundered, and closed the door. The blighters were all creeping back to the rendezvous. When we did at last go off into a fitful sleep, in no time it was morning again and concert day, the artist feeling as though she hadn't slept a wink during the entire night.

Calls from the organiser warning us that there would be a very small audience. Although the auditorium was completely sold out the weather, colder than Minneapolis had ever known, would prevent many people making the journey. We ourselves managed to get to the concert hall without too much difficulty, and when we arrived, discovered the place almost three-quarters full. We couldn't believe our eyes. We did the first of the two programmes here, which we repeat in Chicago. Beginning with Schubert, Schumann and Mahler, with Strauss and Gounod after the interval. I like to give organisers a choice, and usually devise one programme which is designed for a certain kind of audience and a second which is suitable for another kind; it is then up to the individual managements to choose the programme which they think their audience will enjoy most. I sang well; Martin played well. They seemed to enjoy us, and have asked us back as soon as we can make it. So it was a heart-warming start to the tour.

Monday *11 January* We rang the airport early to see how many hours delay we would face on our Chicago flight. Amazingly, everything was working quite normally and we arrived on time in bright sunshine but with terribly low temperatures. The Drake, an old hotel overlooking the Lake, is a familiar friend, so settling in was not traumatic. The rooms have 'closets', that marvellous American clothes cupboard which you walk into and has all the space in the world. Sheer heaven. When we went down to the lobby to deposit my jewellery, which I never keep in my room, there was water cascading over the furniture and lovely carpet; a water main had burst and we must now use the service elevators for the time being.

Tuesday *12 January* People often ask me why I don't use one accompanist exclusively, as so many singers do. I don't believe it is as

77

common a practice as it used to be many years ago, but although it has never been my wish to work only with one pianist I now do most of my work with a very small number: Martin Isepp, Geoffrey Parsons and Geoffrey Pratley and occasionally with Philip Ledger, Graham Johnson and David Owen Norris. One of the great joys of my profession is exchange of ideas; when one is involved with recital repertoire it is extremely interesting to perform, say, Schumann's *Frauenliebe und Leben*, with different people. The combination alters, the interpretation does too, because the human chemistry changes. A different light is shed on a piece just because the human element is different. There is, of course, a great security about working with someone I know, especially when putting together a completely new programme. Martin's strength is his understanding of, and feeling for, the lieder repertoire, which he plays with great sensitivity.

The concerts and recordings I did with Gerald Moore came, sadly, towards the end of his career, and are a shining memory for me. In spite of our joint reputation for extreme leg-pull, for which we were notorious in the recording studios, I always knew he had absolute respect for what I did. When we had recorded a song and were walking out of the studio he would sometimes say very quietly so that no one else could hear, 'I've never heard that sung better.' I could not reply to a remark like that from him; it was the utmost accolade anyone could have. When we actually arrived at the play-back room, his words would be, 'Well, she's quite a promising singer, this girl, she ought to take it up professionally,' or some such remark! I think what pleased Gerald so much was the fact that an English singer had a respected reputation in countries like Germany and France, which do not usually take seriously a foreigner singing their repertoire to them in their language. Gerald was well aware of the regard in which I was held abroad. He and his wife Enid are two of our closest friends.

Occasionally conductors have played for me, Daniel

Barenboim, Raymond Leppard and André Previn. In a recently published book about André I am quoted as saying conductors make far better partners than regular accompanists. I have never in my life said any such thing; I *have* said that the experience is *different*. Conductors are naturally capable of sustaining a feeling of unity for long periods of time. They are used to grasping scores in two ways – horizontally, and in the case of a full orchestra score, vertically as well. Put a piano score in front of them and they see textures and relate them to different instruments, bringing out various colours in the sounds which one might not usually hear. This kind of reading does not make them better accompanists, but it does make the musical experience very rich. The conductors I mentioned are also solo pianists and it is interesting to see how in certain notoriously difficult songs, the technical problems do not seem to exist! Conductors also treat bar lines in another way, they allow them to disappear altogether. Bar lines chop up a phrase visually, and it is a great temptation to allow the mind to hesitate for a fraction of a second when you see one on a page. It's a trap which good conductors avoid, with the result that the music moves forward in an uninterrupted flow. For them, too, no bar is ever the same tempo all the way through. Because of the necessity to deal with and coordinate different instruments, there is a magical ebb and flow going on all the time as one part of the orchestra compensates for another, and the conductor's right hand keeps the basic tempo of a piece under control. Bringing the same techniques and outlook to a song broadens the possibilities greatly.

Thursday
14 January The Chicago concert went well last night. A warmly appreciative audience in a huge auditorium, not an ideal place for a recital. We repeated the Minneapolis programme, so there was no rehearsal to do; although this is the first time I have done these

79

groups of songs in this particular order I am discovering through performing them, which is, of course, the only way to find out, that it is an excellent programme, constructed with a deliberate attempt to juxtapose songs of varying mood and tempo. However well it looks on paper, the only test of a good programme is in actual performance. This one makes me feel as though I am standing on a well-balanced rock!

Sir Georg Solti is here on the same floor of our hotel, and as we leave for Ann Arbor tomorrow we are free to listen to him conducting one of the best orchestras in the world tonight. Beyond a certain level, comparisons are not only odious, but quite pointless. The great orchestras, like all great performers, are equal, but different. People love to compare performances too, and it seems to me such a waste of time. The whole essence of music is that it happens 'Now'. This 'Now' is made up of different elements, artist, hall, audience, weather, country, time of day – all sorts of things which will never be exactly the same again. The performance is always unique; the universe changes, moment by moment; nothing stands still. A piece of music, which comes to life for its moment, also cannot stand still, it can never be the same twice. It is this perpetual growth, development, and movement which I find so fascinating when I sing certain pieces over and over again, to find them altered each time. The aspect which worries me about recorded music is that a recording is frozen in time. When people, as they often do, compare a live performance including all its inevitable faults and failings, with a static one on a tape or disc, they have their priorities the wrong way round. It should always be remembered that the reality, the changing living reality of a moment in performance, is the true one; a photograph is not a living person, a record is not a living performance, only a reminder. Everything about music has to do with duration in time; time is its most important aspect. As soon as any note is sounded it begins to disappear, the 'tempo' or 'speed' of a work is perhaps the most important factor of its structure. It is usually the first piece of information the composer gives to us on the score. In live music there are a number of different times which have to be coincided; the composer is 'past' time because his work is already done, the performers and the individuals in the audience are present time, one breathes life into the score the other listens. There is also future time, as the work reveals itself moment by moment until it is finished. We therefore have a remarkable example of music as a fourth dimension, containing within it the elements of past, present, and future. This is one of the reasons it has such power over those who love it.

Recordings have one vital element missing. The 'present' of the interpreters is frozen – it cannot move, develop, or change. Of course, recorded music has its own special, vital place in our lives. What worries me is the tendency to judge living performances by recorded ones, instead of the other way round. So called 'technical perfection' seems out of place to me. The human experience and the world of Nature contain an element of risk, of error, of unpredictability. The possibility of something new, or of change, is closely bound together with the idea of life. Take away that possibility and you have something different, which shouldn't be confused with the living reality. Recording will always have an important role to play – for those who can't get to hear the real thing, for those who want to study. But if people expect to hear in the concert hall the same precision of balance between the various sections of an orchestra, or between an orchestra and a soloist, they are bound to be disappointed. If someone comes round to the Green Room after one of my performances and begins to compare my interpretation with that on another occasion, or with a recording they might have heard, it tells me immediately that they haven't been listening. In the marvellous moment of performance there is absolutely no room for anything else at all *except that moment* and if one misses it, it's gone for ever. Sadly, most of our lives are spent in mulling over

81

the past and wondering about the future. Few of us ever live NOW.

Later: And this is what music is all about, the perfect marriage between a conductor and orchestra of the first rank. The understanding between Solti and the Chicago Symphony has reached such a pitch that they seem to communicate by telepathy. Solti's gestures are of the utmost refinement – he gives the instrumentalists what looks and sounds like unlimited freedom but his mind and body bind all the forces securely into a marvellous unity. When the music is progressing quite easily he hardly uses any gesture; one can see the tip of the baton giving a clear beat, and sometimes that poetic left hand shaping the phrase. But watch him when a change of tempo or a tricky passage for a specific section is imminent. He gathers himself together, and one can see him not only guiding the players physically, but willing them with all his might to come through the passage perfectly. Since Orchestra Hall has been improved acoustically (mind you, it was superb before) the musicians can hear each other effortlessly; an ensemble of a hundred players has the precision of a string quartet. And it all looks so *easy*. Great art always does. Due to impeccable rehearsing and hugely talented instrumentalists the technical difficulties are left somewhere in outer space. What the audience hears is music-making and interpretation at such a level that we are aware only of sublime music played with joy. The hall was full of joy tonight and we all left with it oozing out of our ears.

We joined the maestro in his suite for the most relaxed and enjoyable supper imaginable. A small group of his friends had arranged the food, together with Charles Kaye, Sir Georg's secretary. When we went in, there was Georg holding court in a large wing chair, basking in their affection and admiration and having a wonderful time. It is marvellous to see him conduct. It is equally so to be in his company and hear him talk about his orchestra. He knows very well how privileged he is to be in charge of one of the two finest orchestras in the world. He also

82

knows what a tremendous price he has to pay in personal terms, often having to leave his wife and daughters behind in England, in order to spend time in Chicago. Those who have seen him with his children can perhaps begin to guess how great that price is for him. Those who hear his music with the orchestra can only be utterly grateful that he is willing to pay it. What a happy evening, and what an ending to our time in this great city.

Friday
15 January
A weekend in the country; Ann Arbor, near Detroit – an unspoiled university town, not a skyscraper in sight; just little shops with original fronts, clustered round the main campus square, with good bookshops, restaurants and students everywhere. It has a special atmosphere and seems somehow apart, in the way that Oxford and Cambridge are. Life is different in such places. Much of Ann Arbor's style is in the old wooden houses at the heart of the campus; the young people who live in them walk past us on the street, full of purpose, clear-eyed and serious. Most of the staff in our hotel are students. They are very patient and good-tempered, even when our simple breakfast order is wrong twice running, and we are irritated! The concert hall holds four thousand, has wonderful acoustics and luxurious dressing rooms. Everything in the garden seems lovely. And then during dinner the thing I dread most of all, an allergic attack, suddenly strikes me down. I have suffered this curse for about ten years; in the space of a few minutes my face swells, distorting my eyes, nose, mouth, throat membrane, until I look like some grotesque monster. It is very frightening and I have to go to bed immediately, dosed with anti-histamine. The worry would not be so overwhelming had I not a public deadline to make. There is no way I can sing in such a physical state; no way I can allow anyone to see my poor face in such a horrifying condition. This attack is severe and will take about five days to subside. Today is Friday; Sunday afternoon at 4 p.m. I am due on stage. I lie in

83

bed, miserable, worried, wondering why on earth this cruel, unpredictable visitation has to make life so hard for me?

Saturday 16 January   The organiser has sent an allergist round to the hotel. This is a good place in which to be ill! Dr Preuss attends the head of the singing department in the Faculty of Music and he has assured me he will have me on stage tomorrow afternoon. He has started me on a short course of cortisone and we have had a valuable talk about my condition generally. What emerges from our conversation is precisely what we have known for a long time – that it is practically impossible to isolate all the causes, or combination of causes, which trigger off an attack. Already my diet is of the utmost simplicity; I do not drink alcohol, have recently given up coffee, and avoid like the plague the known items which I have been able to trace. I cannot put a finger on the culprit this time; I drank some chlorinated water, half a glass, at dinner, but Dr Preuss doesn't think that could have done it. Anyway, the good news is that I shall be fit to perform tomorrow.

Sunday 17 January   My face is improved but by 4 p.m., although I am ready to go on to the platform, my energy level is low and I look as though I have walked into two lamp-posts. It could be worse. Will-power has taken me through a lot of concerts in my time and it will take me through this one.

We do, in fact, have a good concert. I am helped by Martin, the lovely hall, and the warm audience, so I relax and carry on. Our programme changes today; we have an early Italian group and two English ones, although the Mahler and Gounod remain. It is perhaps an easier one to listen to, but every song is,

84

in its own way, beautiful. The acoustics are superb. I am lucky this year; every hall in which I'm appearing is good for sound with Washington and New York outstanding in this respect. The Green Room is packed with people afterwards, friendly, outgoing, full of enthusiasm for us and the programme.

Straight back to bed and a quiet dinner brought to my room, while Keith and Martin dine downstairs.

Monday We breakfasted, packed, paid our bill, and then had a free half-
18 January hour to walk in the fresh air. It really was fresh in Ann Arbor, and although still bitingly cold, we were well wrapped-up and enjoyed treading in the crisp, hard snow. My face still badly marked and noticeably swollen, but my dark glasses hide the worst of it.

Our journey to St. Louis was uneventful; warmer temperatures and bright sun greeted us. We stood outside the hotel with our faces lifted towards it, basking in the light. A quick, late lunch and a long walk before the sun set. There was a large park opposite the hotel and we made for it straight away. After about half an hour the sun began to fade; it grew colder; no one was around. Then a car drew up and stopped near us. Its two occupants looked at us in what appeared to be a highly menacing manner; one of them opened the door of the car, got out, and walked purposefully towards us. We immediately headed straight for the nearest exit, to the main road, and people. We looked over our shoulders to see what the man was up to, and saw him bending over a frozen pond examining the thickness of the ice. At a safe distance we presumed we had been utterly wrong in assuming the men had any suspect intentions towards us. But the fear such an encounter produced was a shocking experience and a sad comment on life not only in the U.S.A., but anywhere in the world these days.

85

Tuesday
19 January

A gruelling morning, talking my head off to journalists and radio interviewers; just the thing I should *not* be doing on my day's rest, I should be absolutely quiet. In order to help the sponsor of the series, an old friend, Jim Cain, I agreed to do it. Jim, one of the kindest, most good-natured people in the business and beloved of many, many artists, was manager of the St. Louis Symphony Orchestra for some years. He now works for the Conservatory of Music and is trying to build up a first class recital series. The school, entirely supported by private patrons, needs a great deal of money each year in order to survive. To this end, we also agreed to attend a dinner given at the home of committee members to meet the Board, and generally try to encourage interest in the recital series. I find it a great strain talking to strangers in smoke-filled rooms, but sometimes it has to be done. In such gatherings there is always at least one person who is a joy to meet, someone who *understands*, and tonight was no exception; the person in question happened to be the Dean of the School, and a more sensitive, intelligent and giving person it would be hard to find.

Wednesday
20 January

We spent some time down by the river front in the museum under the famous St Louis Arch, a modern miracle of engineering, hundreds of feet high and a remarkable, imaginative landmark which attracts large numbers of visitors every year. The museum, underground, has many interesting exhibits; a plough, a sod dwelling, a stage-coach, a stuffed bear and buffalo, and for me the most beautiful thing I've seen in America this year – a tee-pee made of buffalo hide. There is something unbearably beautiful, simple, and moving about this natural dwelling; I could live in one quite easily. The furs on the floor look extremely comfortable, the softness of the hides encourages one to stroke the walls and the proportions are so pleasing to the eye. Since the piles were about twenty feet high at

86

the apex the structure did not seem in the least claustrophobic. When one thinks of the refinement of the Red Indian culture, the sophistication of their religion, the beauty of their artifacts, the nobility of their features, the tragedy of their race is heart breaking, a fact which many Americans realise only too well. The mind reels before the vision of this enormous country undisturbed by modern man, peopled by men who lived with and respected Nature. We should have let *them* civilise *us*.

Lunch on one of the paddle-steamers permanently moored on the river bank, then back to rest before the concert.

I heard that there was a Labrador dog in the audience this evening: his owner, a blind student, upon being asked by an usher whether she ought to take him into the hall, replied smartly, 'He's better behaved than most people!' She was right, too; he sat there as good as gold.

Friday 22 January Washington. We fly in over the city for the last half-hour through a thick belt of fog. Every passenger must think of the Florida flight which crashed last week as they land or take off. Our taxi driver shows us the actual crash spot as we drive past the Fourteenth Street Bridge; it is very close to the end of the runway.

We are in Georgetown, a delightful suburb, no tall buildings, just narrow streets, pretty houses, good restaurants, and deep snow. It reminds me of home. A quiet dinner with two friends who live here, and an early night.

Saturday 23 January Our concert in the Kennedy Centre is sold out with standing room only. That's a good start. The hall is superb acoustically, a building of great beauty. This is the third time I have sung here; before the Centre was built concerts used to be held in an older hall, Constitution, also marvellous for music.

87

In spite of the appalling weather (which has dogged our footsteps for the entire tour) most of the large audience struggled through the snow for the concert. I have always enjoyed appearing in Washington, but tonight there was something special about the warmth of those who had come to hear me and the depth of the silence with which they listened, the sort of silence which is the greatest possible compliment to an artist. For two hours we enjoyed the ultimate in communication; performers, audience, and music were one. There is no way to describe the feelings which arise from this unity nor can we control in any way the circumstances which make it possible. It is a gift from the gods and one is full of gratitude for the occasions when it happens.

We had marvellous food and company later at the beautiful apartment of Patrick Hayes. Evelyn, his wife, is a fine pianist; Patrick has run Washington Performing Arts Society for years, and has the devotion of many artists. I am particularly glad to be here this season which is his last before retirement. A special day.

Sunday New York; for sixteen years the place which has held the most
24 January precious musical memories of my career. So familiar. So beloved in spite of its problems as a city. We have seen it smothered in uncollected rubbish, brought to a standstill by snow, crippled by strikes, crime-ridden, full of both indescribable poverty and wealth, of ugliness and incomparable beauty. By day, an ageing, faded mess. By night, the loveliest city in the world.

People say to me, 'You always have this special affection for New York audiences. Why?' It is a combination of many things; first, I suppose, because they have such affection for me. I do not mean to suggest for a moment that I feel unappreciated elsewhere, but the Americans show their feelings in a way which is typical of them as a nation, completely uninhibited, open-hearted, and generous. Then, of course, I am in New York only for a very short time. When I walk out onto the Carnegie stage, the overwhelming welcome is their way of saying, 'We're glad to see you back with us again'. New York is the most exciting city in the world in which to know success. There is a glamour about making the grade here; the star system is very much a part of the scene and once Americans have made you one they are loyal until the end. When Sol Hurok (who was my agent in New York until he died) saw the way audiences reacted to me here, he tried very hard indeed to persuade me to take up residence and make my base in America, visiting Europe from time to time. Although I was tempted to do so, I felt I simply could not deny my roots to that extent, but I also saw that he was right in thinking that there is something about the way I perform which gets through to people here, and I wanted to keep on coming. I have made this American tour a regular part of my life since 1967, and have benefited in many ways from the challenge both of singing what my audiences want to hear and persuading them to listen to what I want to sing. It has been a rewarding experience which outweighs all the stress and problems of touring in this enormous country. When these Americans give you their hearts, they give them completely and for always.

The next three days will be busy. We have many friends here and usually see some of them for every single meal, including breakfast.

Our hotel on West 54th Street is small and quiet and has the kind of atmosphere which suits us best, friendly, highly convenient, and totally un-smart. We can walk everywhere we need to be.

Monday My first call this morning was to the shop where I buy all my
25 January trousers; pure wool and beautifully cut. I always stock up when I'm here. So we walked right up Madison Avenue to the

89

Women's Haberdashers, where I tried on some clothes, bought some pants, and was presented with a leather bag by the owner. Then to the Carlyle, one block away, where we had invited Raymond (Leppard) to join us for lunch. Full marks to the head waiter who beamed at me, and asked if it was really me! Amazing, since I had my turban and my glasses on, and thought myself totally unrecognisable. Nice talk with Ray, and some useful conversation about *Orfeo* which he is to conduct at Glyndebourne. Keith left us to go and see about my Income Tax; he is up to the eyes in business meetings. Ray and I, clutching each other, slipped and giggled our way to the Metropolitan Museum; we must have made a merry spectacle, but the footpaths are treacherously icy. Consternation and disappointment – the wretched Museum is closed on Monday afternoons, and we turned sadly away. I won't have another opportunity to go there.

Dinner in the evening with a friend whose Fifth Avenue duplex apartment overlooks Central Park. It is hard when we are there to tear ourselves away from the view and go in to dinner. Her dining-room is circular and does amazing things to the speaking voice – Keith, sitting opposite me, sounded like a Russian bass! A lovely, hilarious evening.

Tuesday
26 January
I speak to my father on the phone every few days. He is anxious for us to be home. The various members of the family are so kind to him, as are our neighbours, but it's good to know that he wants us back home as badly as we want to be there with him. I wish I didn't have to leave him, but it is inevitable. Fortunately he is well, and very good about being on his own.

Rehearsed in Carnegie, the hall most beloved in all the world by many artists, and certainly by me. I walk out onto that stage and it is like coming home. The television film crew is here, and we had a good opportunity to plan strategy for tomorrow, when they begin filming.

Lunched with a colleague; Keith at yet another meeting, but joined us halfway through the meal. I slept in the afternoon; I have been sleeping so badly – oh, for my own bed!

Lena Horne in the evening. What can one possibly say about a truly great star? We couldn't take our eyes off her, she has the charisma, the beauty, which only comes from great discipline. The voice, ah! the voice! It sounds fresh, strong, vibrant, youthful, with a tremendous range; her rhythmic sense is beyond praise. I spent half the evening in tears, the other half with prickles up and down my spine. What energy, humour, and can she dance! Everything Julie Andrews said about her is true. In her own sphere she is the equal of the Chicago Symphony in terms of excellence. Thank goodness I didn't miss her.

Wednesday 27 January Carnegie Day! We spent an hour in bitter cold wind being filmed wending our way from the hotel to the hall; what a performance! The crew would take a bit of film, stop us, run on ahead, and do a bit more. During one stop, three strangers came up, one after the other, grabbed me by the arm, beamed, and said, 'Coming to hear you tonight – what are you doing here?' 'Being filmed!' I *like* New Yorkers! We eventually got back inside, frozen stiff, but with everything safely in the can. It is interesting to see how people react to the sight of the camera. They aren't at all interested in the subject: they just edge over until they think they're in shot themselves – a kind of natural reaction, like bees to honey!

Lunch with a friend from Boston, in town for the concert, and then a long rest. We packed, got ready, and the limousine arrived at 7 p.m. I needed to be early in order to practise thoroughly and open all my messages. It's always like Christmas Day in my

91

dressing room here. David Rendall arrived, looking exhausted, bearing greetings and written messages from Kiri, Colin Graham, and Ubaldo Gardini, who had just finished their *Cosi* dress rehearsal at the Met. I was touched by their notes – what a kind thing to do. David soon works with me in *Mary Stuart*, but is in New York until March. And I am going home tomorrow!

And so out on to the stage for the warmest welcome I ever receive. For the past fifteen years I have appeared in recital here, thirteen times in Carnegie itself. Each of those concerts has been a memorable experience, every year has seen a growth in the communication between audience and singer. It is a quite indescribable and unique event for me. Each year I ask myself, 'What if the magic goes tonight?' So far the magic has appeared without fail, and this year, so people tell me, is the best yet. All I know as I stand there reacting to the long tumultuous welcome, looking at the packed house, the packed stage behind me, is that these wonderful open-hearted New Yorkers establish, before I have opened my mouth, the quality of the concert they will hear. They set the standard for me, and all I have to do is give back what they first give to me.

Afterwards I greet the long line of people waiting to see me in the Green Room, so many of them familiar faces which I see every year; then to Harold Shaw's apartment and the annual party he gives for me. I sit in his beautiful drawing-room, where I am fed delectable food and everybody takes turns to keep me company. This evening I feel completely fresh, even after a taxing programme. Harold is the perfect agent; a quiet, understanding gentleman who never pressures me. We couldn't have a better relationship. When it is time to leave, the car takes us straight out to Kennedy Airport where we have decided to spend the night in order to check in by 8 a.m. – this gives us a little more sleeping time. Home tomorrow! One more Carnegie recital is over. I shall be nourished by it for a year until next January.

Thursday
28 January

An uneventful, peaceful flight home. A month of travel and work behind us, a month in which so much has happened that we feel we have been away for an age. We are greeted by my father, so happy to see us back, a beautifully warm and clean house, kept in its usual order by our friend and treasure, Florence, and a huge pile of mail. We decide to walk before going to bed and as we feel the lovely damp gentle English air on our faces it seems like spring to us after the bitter American cold. We like our climate, we like living and being in England more than anywhere else in the world. For work other places are of paramount importance – an international performer has to be an international traveller. But there is no place like home and I do my best to be here as much as I can. So to sleep in my own bed and the first unbroken night since we left.

In our garden

With my father

A favourite
local walk

Overleaf: at home

Part Three

Rotterdam
Cambridge
Copenhagen
Mary Stuart, English National Opera

MARY STUART

Opera in three acts
Italian libretto by Giuseppe Bardari
English translation by Tom Hammond
Music by Gaetano Donizetti
Producer John Copley
Designer Desmond Heeley
Lighting Robert Bryan
Staff Producers Peter Foster, Lesley Lee, Keith Warner
First night of a revival of this production
at the London Coliseum,
1 April 1982

Queen Elizabeth I	Rosalind Plowright
George Talbot, Earl of Shrewsbury	John Tomlinson
Sir William Cecil	Alan Opie
Robert Dudley, Earl of Leicester	David Rendall
Hannah Kennedy	Angela Bostock
Mary Stuart	Janet Baker

English National Opera Chorus
Chorus Master: Leslie Fyson
English National Opera Orchestra
Conductor: Charles Mackerras

Monday After a month of hibernation, my batteries recharged, it is time to
1 March start work again. A pleasant flight to Rotterdam; a flight without
any hitch at all is more unusual than it should be, but even with
the baggage-handling strike at Heathrow, there were no hiccups.
Our plane hit severe turbulence coming in to land. High winds
threw the aircraft about like a piece of balsa-wood. The pilot
brought us down very fast, it seemed, and although neither of us
is nervous of flying we were glad to be on the ground.

After dinner we walked about the deserted streets. In the dark
the town looks like a hundred others on the Continent which
were flattened during the last war. Although I was only eleven
when war finished it must have left a really deep impression on
my childhood. Those six years fascinate me, especially when I
travel in Europe. I wonder for instance, how the once-occupied
peoples feel when I sing to them in German?

Tuesday In broad daylight and bright sunshine we got a better
2 March perspective of this place. The Dutch, like so many nations, love
greenery; the rather faceless buildings have the saving grace of
being a comfortable proportion to which the human body can
relate. Tall buildings seem to me overwhelming in every sense;
these Rotterdam streets give an impression of cosiness and have
the added bonus of carefully planted trees, open spaces, seats
and flower-beds. In the summer it must be delightful. Already
we are aware of a marked slowing down; life here is obviously led
at a calmer, more gentle pace than London. We walked to the
Doelen Hall to meet Geoffrey Pratley, who is accompanying me
for the first concert, a recital. The Doelen is that rarity, a modern
hall with excellent acoustics. I have been here only once before,

although a regular visitor to the Concertgebouw in Amsterdam, but even on that occasion I remember vividly how impressed I was by the sound. Right outside the stage door is a heart-warming sight. The Dutch town dwellers are determined to remind themselves that the countryside is not far away, and in between the large railway station, flanked by a busy road with heavy traffic pouring along it, we saw a fenced-off farmyard! I can describe it in no other way. There it was, a large greenish-brown patch of grass and mud with a shelter and pens filled with hay for all the animals walking about enjoying the sunshine. There were ducks (but no pond!) goats, sheep with a few babies, and some sweet little fawns who were playing at follow-my-leader around the perimeter and paying not the slightest attention to two gawping and delighted foreigners. The rehearsal room looked out over this scene and I found it difficult to concentrate. We had done most of our rehearsing at home, though, and really only needed to remind ourselves of tempi.

A good lunch, then a sleep and back to the hall by 7.45. The audience was rather a shock; my last concert was Carnegie Hall and as always I find the transition from the vociferous immediate response of Americans so very different from that anywhere else. It is interesting how audiences take on completely different characteristics. One generalises about the warmth of Mediterranean people, the cooler temperament of Northern Europeans, but in a curious way, a group in an auditorium does reflect a little of the national colour of a country, and the Dutch are calm, without flamboyance, full of respect and listen quietly. I find it difficult if I am not getting some feed-back; performing is, I believe, such a two-way communication. However, by the interval they were on their feet applauding. In the second half I had become used to their brand of response, and we had a happy evening.

Geoffrey is due to leave us in the morning. I have known and worked with this gentle, hard-working and utterly conscientious man for many years. He is on the staff at the Royal Academy but does a great deal of work outside. He always comes to first rehearsals totally prepared and usually has all the music too, even in the obscure keys I sometimes use. His particular gift is in the English repertoire, which he somehow manages to invest with a beauty and significance which isn't always there. Our programme here contained a group of early Italian songs which we have done together before, but not for a long time. He had not forgotten a single thing about my performance of them when we came to rehearse. Like Martin, he is an easy and friendly person to travel with, never out of sorts, always helpful, with an unfailingly high standard of performance.

Wednesday We woke to torrential rain and black skies. This week I am
3 March singing every day, either performing or rehearsing; now that the recital is behind me, I do two performances of *Das Lied von der Erde* on Thursday and Friday. The scheduled conductor is sick and we have a young Polish musician to take over.

After a quiet day mostly spent indoors due to the abominable weather, we met at six p.m. for a thorough piano rehearsal together with the tenor, Keith Lewis, whom I had not met before. The facilities at the Doelen are luxurious, with large spaces, good pianos, comfortable chairs, even an anteroom with a bed to lie down on, and a spotlessly clean bathroom. We each have a suite like this, and I occupy the same one I used yesterday for the recital, which looks out over the animals. I am old enough to be the conductor's mother and though he treats me with the utmost respect, I feel I must be very careful to accord him the same courtesy. No matter what his age, he is the person with the stick and in control of the situation. Keith Lewis is performing the work for the first time and it is obvious from the moment he opens his mouth that he has not only a very good voice but has done meticulous preparation. We went right through the piece, a heavy sing for both of us, and then straight onto the platform without a break to meet the orchestra. We then proceeded to go through it all again; it was necessary to use full voice since rehearsing with an orchestra for the brief time available to put a work together entails achieving some sort of balance immediately, and I could not hold back, although I felt very much like doing so after my recital last night. By the time nine o'clock arrived we had rehearsed solidly and without a pause, and I was thankful to hear we were not needed after the tea break. There was some good playing from the orchestra; it sounded as though they had played the score many times which is a tremendous help since *Das Lied* is an exposed work for all concerned.

We walked back to the hotel through empty streets the skies clear of rain. The invigorating air in Rotterdam is a constant reminder that one is not far from the sea.

I was very tired; my lungs ached from hours of deep breathing and the effort of projecting over a large orchestra. Keith, of course, noticed my fatigue, and asked me which was the greater, mental or physical tiredness? I couldn't answer; they were, in this instance so totally inseparable. I thought of my young colleague just starting his career; I wouldn't want to change places with him. I wouldn't want to change places with anyone for that matter, or alter my own experience one jot. I suspect that to make such a statement at all must mean *something* but I'm not quite sure what!

Thursday 4 March There is a huge booming clock outside the hotel. It strikes all the quarter hours but is for most of the day about three-quarters of an hour late. Then in the afternoon it starts to catch up on itself, and the next time one looks it is only ten minutes out. A most curious state of affairs.

The weather has brightened up so we intend to explore a bit. On Tuesday there was a large hurdy-gurdy in the shopping precinct near-by, playing such captivating tunes that we felt like grabbing each others' arms and doing a wild waltz in and out of the shoppers. Not exactly the normal behaviour of two middle-aged English visitors – but tempting all the same.

We put our heads out of the hotel and down came the rain. Nevertheless we had to have some exercise and plodded about feeling a bit miserable, taking refuge from time to time in shops.

By using a mink coat (which had become unfashionably short) as a lining to a French raincoat, I now possess one of the most useful garments I have ever had in my wardrobe; a warm coat, (warm enough for a Canadian winter) which is also water-proof. I have worn it far more than as a fur coat only, and can brave terrible weather without worrying too much. Even so, we could only take a certain amount this morning before giving up and coming back to our cage once again.

The concert this evening was beautiful. Keith Lewis acquitted himself very well indeed. He did not fall into the trap of trying to compete with an impossible orchestration in the first song, but sang within his capacity. I believe he will have a most rewarding career.

Although I do not have the voice for certain composers, Verdi, Wagner and Puccini, for instance, at least to be plunged into the world of Mahler is more than ample compensation. There could not be a more satisfying experience than to embark upon the heavenly, soaring phrases written for the mezzo voice in *Das Lied*. I enjoyed myself so much tonight and the orchestra played marvellously.

Home to a quiet supper in our room and later a walk in the deserted streets. It had stopped raining – at last! My father told me when I telephoned him that it had been a beautiful day in London!

Saturday Up at 5.15 to catch the early plane back to London. It is no effort
6 March to rise at such an hour when London is the destination! Our final
day in Rotterdam yesterday brought clearer skies, a great relief. I
would very much like to see this town in summer when people
are sitting under the lovely trees, drinking coffee and eating
pastries.

The second performance of *Das Lied* last night was broadcast,
and after we had finished and said goodbye to everyone we came
back to our room to pack in readiness for our early start today. We
have refused all supper invitations here because after singing, the
last thing I want to do is sit around a table and talk for two hours,
especially as I have done three performances in four days. People
in the profession usually understand this perfectly; it is sometimes
difficult for those outside it to realise how hard singers work their
vocal chords. Talking is such a natural function, but to employ this
function after one has been singing is for many of us the straw
which breaks the camel's back! I try not to do it, but inevitably,
kind would-be hosts are sometimes a little puzzled and hurt. I do
my duty faithfully on those occasions when my appearance is
absolutely necessary.

As usual, we sit in the aeroplane feeling that the days since last
Monday have spanned weeks. But it is now Saturday, we are on
the way home, it is a beautiful morning and I don't have to sing
again until Monday.

An incident occurred yesterday which interested me deeply.
Late in the afternoon a large and vociferous group of
demonstrators stood outside the hotel waving banners and
chanting slogans for hours on end. We were told this was a
demonstration against the American Ambassador, who was
somewhere in the building. The sight of the crowd, the ugliness
of it all, the presence of police, and the sound of shouting was
disturbing, particularly in the context of the calm and gentleness
of the Dutch people we had met. The demonstrators were
apparently not Dutch.

I wondered if the Ambassador could hear it; whether he was so used to this kind of behaviour that it didn't bother him any more, or whether he also found it deeply disturbing. And I went on to think about the difficulties surrounding other people's lives and work. Mostly, I am totally pre-occupied with my own problems, but of course we all have to cope, at least to some extent, with negative aspects. These may be confined to home, school, office or place of work, but they are definitely a part of everybody's life. The thing about the life of a public person is that a great many people know about his circumstances because the media publicises them, and often in a distorted form.

Last summer I was asked to give a perfectly straightforward interview to a journalist, in connection with opera performances in which I happened to be involved. In the course of the interview I mentioned, in reply to a question about future plans, that after July 1982 I would not be doing any more operatic performances.

The next day, to my utter consternation, the interview was printed giving prime importance to that one remark, and the journalist went so far as to suggest that I had summoned him to my house to give him first crack at this – in order that I could announce to the world the news of my impending retirement from the theatre! Nothing could be further from the truth. Since it was, and is, my intention to carry on with my other work, I honestly did not believe that the decision to quit opera would be of undue interest to anyone other than the theatre managements, who are, of course, concerned with long-term planning and need to have this information. But the damage was done, and many other newspapers picked up the item. The article has caused a spotlight to be placed on my opera appearances this year, something which I wished to have avoided completely. The word 'retirement' also has a misleading connotation and I constantly receive letters from members of the public expressing sadness at the fact that I am to sing no more! The situation has arisen solely because of a piece of irresponsible reporting, and is not of my own making. I am even accused of arranging endless farewell performances, just because I am returning to each of the houses with which I have been involved over the years. I have, I believe, every right to say 'goodbye' to all my friends in the theatre. It is unfortunate that the fact of these final operatic performances has been so exaggerated, but I have to live with it, the American Ambassador has to cope with the demonstrators, the man-in-the street has somehow to rise above the irritations of daily life.

It is an interesting fact that although performers do not normally have the power to defend themselves against anything which is written about them or correct it, at this moment I am in the unusual position of having a pen in my hand and I can at least give *my* version of the situation which has arisen. If I claim to be such a private person by nature, it might well be asked why I am writing this book! I do not want a stranger producing a book about me. If there is anything worth publishing about either me or my life, then surely it had better come straight from the horse's mouth!

Ever since I can remember, I have been passionately interested in the written word. Books are my life, together with music. The power and beauty of the written word is, to me, a sacred responsibility. What I am writing here is the truth as I see it, and I believe no-one can know my personal truth as clearly and honestly as I myself. It is said that we all have a book inside us, well, here is mine!

Wednesday 10 March We drove through a rain-swept landscape to Cambridge. I had offered, ages ago, to sing a performance of the St. Matthew Passion in King's College Chapel for my old friend and colleague Philip Ledger, just for the sheer joy of doing such music in such a place.

The event had been arranged and the entire operation

organised to fit into one day, no small matter since the rehearsing schedule alone is extremely difficult to complete within the time allowed, and we were doing a full performance in German.

We arrived at King's after a brief picnic lunch in a Cambridge lane and started work immediately. Philip had agreed to rehearse all my numbers at one fell swoop in order to give me a chance to rest before we began Part I at 5.30 p.m. Philip is not only an accompanist and continuo player of the highest order (we have done most enjoyable recitals together) but also a really remarkable choir trainer.

The orchestra, mostly university students, was of a high standard; Philip's clear beat and general grasp of the score and its difficulties ensured a smooth passage. The only problem was the building itself. The day was showery and the light kept changing constantly. Confronting me was the West Window, rich in fabulous colours, and on either side of the nave smaller expanses of glass which because of the light, put on an extraordinary display of fireworks, absolutely breathtaking in its beauty. And there I was trying my best to sing with that exhibition of colours smack in my face!

I was given a charming suite in the Provost's house where I could rest and change, a most attractive place. Cambridge is full of such lodgings; the Master's Lodge at Trinity, for instance, where we have stayed with Sir Alan and Lady Hodgkin on occasions, must be the most beautiful of them all. I can imagine the sadness of a tenancy like that one coming to its inevitable end, but the opportunity to live surrounded by such splendour must enrich one spiritually, no matter for how short a time. The room where I rested today was painted in a lovely deep mushroom with white paintwork and lampshades, peaceful and gentle on the eye.

5.30 arrived and the performers met in Philip's room before walking together into the Chapel, packed with people.

As the first sublime bars of music began, I realised that the

107

building had dressed itself in quite different garments from those of the afternoon. It was dark, so the glass ceased to dominate; instead the bare-bones, the skeleton, emerged; soft lights at intervals along the wall brought out the simple strength of the warm stone and showed off to perfection the splendour of the fan vaulting. I sat, totally overwhelmed both by the stunning visual impact, and the structure of Bach's writing, the only sound which could ever stand as an equal partner in these circumstances. It was as if the Chapel understood exactly what the occasion was all about and had decided to set the proper scene for the music. The result was a meeting of the senses at the kind of level one experiences rarely, and as the first part of the Passion unfolded, I knew that the evening would be filed away in my mind as an event of the most special kind.

At seven we broke for one and a half hours and the soloists, together with Philip and my Keith, were given a sensibly chosen dinner in a warm and welcoming room. We ate melon, salad and syllabub; I opted out of the last course. It is tricky to have to eat in the middle of this work. My singing is mostly in the second half so I can't fill myself with food because my breath control suffers.

The break passed quickly and as we returned for Part II, I decided to put on yet another layer, my velvet cloak, because we had been very cold in Chapel.

The fresh young voices of the choir were incredibly touching, the great arias and the poignant simplicity of the Evangelist's phrases all sounded at their very best, as mellow as the golden walls which wrapped themselves around the music we made. I sat on a small platform with the three other soloists involved in the arias, Kathleen Livingstone, William Kendall, and Gerald Finley. They were all young people with their careers ahead of them. The accomplished style which they had already achieved was amazing; all had superb voices, all sang very well indeed. I thought how firm and sure is the fate of our profession with youngsters like these around and I felt proud of them. On the other side of the conductor, as is the custom, another platform held the Evangelist and Christus, Ian Partridge and Stephen Roberts, colleagues with whom I have worked many times before.

Their inspired 'conversation' was full of beautiful and moving moments. My cup, as they say, was full, and I sat there, in great happiness to be a part of it all.

We came to the phrase where the choir sings 'Truly this was the Son of God'. For me, these few bars contain everything which music can possibly say; Bach has summed up in music which lasts only seconds, the entire feeling to which human sense can aspire.

To hear these bars at least once a year, gives my life a focus which it would otherwise not contain. My work has taken me into many different spheres, and composers. These eight bars bring me back home where I belong, to the Church music which has been a part of me for as long as I can remember; the first music I ever sang and probably the last. At the end of the performance Philip put down his baton and there was a silence.

Such a silence I have never experienced before. Then the audience rose to its feet and we soloists walked slowly down the nave and out of the door.

After the usual affectionate 'goodbyes' had been said, we drove quietly back to London. A brilliantly full moon was shining. A rare event is occurring up there in the heavens right now. All the major planets are in the same quadrant of the sky, something which will not happen again until 2357. This important conjunction has caused predictions of catastrophe and doom from the astrologers. But why do they not suppose that to balance the gloom, at this moment events of equal felicity must also be possible? After all, we took part in one tonight!

Sunday
14 March The tall, distinguished figure of Geoffrey Parsons came towards us as we waited at the gate for the Copenhagen flight. His easygoing, friendly and charming personality disguises one of the great artists of our time.

I first met Geoffrey many years ago when I was about twenty-four. I found him so intimidating! His life seemed to arrange itself without any trouble at all; he was surrounded by helpful friends, his career was developing well, he didn't have any apparent problems and when he sat down at the keyboard my first thought was: Anyone who makes it sound *that* easy can't be any good! My own nervous, retiring, unsure disposition must have made me seem like a country mouse to him!

We have worked together ever since and I have watched him gradually turn from an immensely gifted young man into an artist of the very first rank. Geoffrey really does have everything. His outgoing, friendly Australian personality, full of common sense, makes him a joy to be with. He is a tremendous worker and this is an especially endearing trait, because technically he is perhaps the most outstanding accompanist of his generation with the facility and ease which would persuade a lesser person that work isn't necessary. I respect this attitude more than I can say. Because instruments vary so much in concert halls, (most of them are under par) it is essential for the accompanist to get to know the piano very quickly indeed. At least singers take around with them their own instrument! The pianist often has to overcome all sorts of difficulties and the only way to do so is to practise. Geoffrey's technique is so sure, he could probably get away with very little effort of this particular kind, but I do not know anyone who works harder than he does, either before we rehearse at home, or actually on the day of the concert, wherever we happen to be.

Geoffrey's speed of reaction ensures that he is following my phrasing but it is much more than accompanying; he actually feels a great deal of the music we perform together in exactly the same way I do, and we can hear each other going in the same direction, or receding from the peak of a phrase in the same way. There is discussion, of course, but not so much of that: it just isn't necessary. We have watched each other grow and develop as artists all these years, we have both achieved positions at the top of our professions and more important, we have stayed there. I stand on a platform with Geoffrey in total security. The technical difficulty of some songs, the notorious accompaniment of Mendelssohn's *Hexenlied* for instance, holds no fear for him, neither does the different problem of a song like the Schubert setting of *Die junge Nonne*. Such freedom means that interpretation can begin on a high level. The one factor which is of prime importance to me is rhythm. Rhythm is the basic architecture of a song, without it, the building is founded on sand instead of rock. Once the rhythm of the phrase is secure within that framework one can do all sorts of things without destroying the shape; the differences which happen each time are the moments which make music eternally fresh and exciting.

Finding the perfect accompanist is like finding the perfect teacher – an entirely individual and practically impossible task.

But when it happens – miraculous! The perfect teacher (or accompanist) is only so for a limited number of people. The most famous teacher of singing will only be able to 'teach' a relatively few pupils because the relationship is a deeply psychological one; teacher and pupil can relate at depth because they strike a deep response in each other, and this is never possible with everybody. So with accompanist and singer. Geoffrey will play superbly for all his artists, but perhaps the degree he himself enters into the interpretation will depend on the musical affinity he feels with each individual. From my point of view our collaboration is as fulfilling and rewarding as it could be. My recital programmes are planned to give maximum differences of range, style and language, in all areas Geoffrey is equally strong and in my experience reveals no weaknesses of any kind either technical or interpretative.

The equivalent of this amazing talent would be a singer who could sing every single role in the repertoire equally well! I just don't know of one! I mentioned that Geoffrey in his early years gave the impression of the world falling easily into his lap. I am quite certain he must have had problems as he struggled to make a place in our profession. He was extremely careful not to burden his singers with those problems and probably believed it to be his duty to provide an unflappable, unworried, smiling countenance in order to spare the already nervous performer even more anxiety. He still does the same, and presents himself in my music room, on an aeroplane or in a concert hall as a person at the complete service of his artist, leaving his private concerns at home. I hope he feels something of the gratitude one singer at least has towards him; gratitude for him as a person and the most enormous respect and love for him as an artist.

Hanne, one of the Hansen sisters who have been my Danish agents for many years, met us at the airport and drove us to the Angleterre which has changed hands since we were last there. I itched to get hold of a Hoover and give the lobby carpet a jolly good clean; there are workmen in the building causing a great deal of dust. The town clock proceeded to play a merry tune of welcome at midnight, but then decided to shut up for the rest of the night.

Copenhagen has been very kind to me. I have visited this clean, breezy town many times. Three years ago I was awarded the Danish Sonning Prize for outstanding service to the musical profession. My heart warms to the Danes when I think, as I inevitably do here, of the incident during the war when the King and everyone else wore yellow stars as moral support to the Jewish community. Marvellous!

Geoffrey had already worked in a studio by the time we met to go to the Tivoli, a large hall in the famous gardens where the concert was to be held. Bodil, a cheerful girl from the Hansen office drove us at breakneck speed through the traffic; she has a tremendous sense of humour. What a lovely thing to be able to crack jokes in another language!

We tested the lights, sang a song or two, viewed the luxurious backstage accommodation and Geoffrey arranged with the stage-manager to come back at 3 p.m. to work on the piano we were to use that evening.

Then a walk, a delicious buffet lunch and sleep, tea at 5.30 p.m. and unhurried preparations for the concert. I wore a new dress for the first time – slipper satin in a vivid green. I gave Keith strict instructions to give me an honest opinion about its impact from the distance, since a dress can change so radically from the back of a large hall. Bodil came to fetch us and as she drove, told us about a remark in the local newspaper which had informed its readers that, regardless of the abominable weather they had been suffering for days, Spring had actually arrived because Janet Baker was in town to sing! I thought that was nice. Half an hour of concentrated warming up, which I can't inflict

113

on hotel guests, but prefer to do in the privacy of my dressing room, then out onto the stage; bright acoustics and a wonderfully warm and friendly audience. A good proportion of them had come out with severe cases of croup! During this series, one artist, a pianist, I believe, had leaned over the piano and said to the audience at some point, 'I can hear you. Can you hear me?' I was luckier: they had a good cough between songs. But what a generous response they gave us and what a very happy night we had. Keith says that he can tell when I'm enjoying myself by the way I come on and walk off. Sometimes there is more bounce than others!

Tuesday 16 March Up at 7 a.m. Ugh! But it's worth it to be at home. After an early lunch and a sleep, Bill from the English National Opera wardrobe department arrived, with his assistants, to fit my *Mary Stuart* costumes. We plied them with tea and honey cake and then proceeded to try on my Act III dress. To my great relief (and theirs) it slipped into the old hooks perfectly. It is always a bad moment for me if my costumes don't feel comfortable; the struggle to keep my weight down is a never-ending battle. The velvet cloak for the final scene has always been a problem because of its weight. For the whole evening I carry the weight of the skirts with their enormous yardage, around my waist; they are tightly fitted but well balanced. At the point of the opera when I have still a lot of big singing to do, I change suddenly into a garment like a long coat, and have to carry that on my shoulders, since it is loose. It is hard to breathe against this new centre of gravity, so today Bill has come prepared with a number of ideas to relieve me of an unnecessary burden. John (Copley) has already given him permission; 'Do whatever she likes, but make her comfortable.' The last thing we all want is to alter the look of the costumes but I hope we can achieve both looks and comfort. My Act II black velvet (a great favourite) is completely

Mary Stuart

new because the original one was given away to raise money for charity. I wonder who has it now? It is a valuable session and we part after two hours feeling the time has been used well and I am easy in my mind.

We drove down to the Merchant Taylors' Hall to rehearse with Sir Georg Solti and a section of the Royal College of Music Orchestra. Valerie, Lady Solti, has asked me to take part in a fund raising effort for the Hampstead Old Peoples' Housing Trust. We eventually found the hall, after tearing our hair out in a tobacconist's shop which had the effrontery to be on the spot we thought we were looking for. The idiosyncracies of the City are unfathomable except to the favoured few who work there. We rehearsed our Mendelssohn piece, with the orchestra in cracking form, and then Sir Georg and I did our three songs with piano which completed my contribution. Valerie was looking distraught but had found the time to go out to Asprey's and buy me a really lovely flower pot holder as a 'thank you'.

There were many people listening, most of them occupied in arranging flowers, or making tea, or being generally useful; Edward Heath popped in because he was making a speech elsewhere that evening and didn't want to miss hearing us. As I left Edward Fox arrived. He was reading poems and I rather thought he would find the hall difficult for the spoken word since it is so outstandingly good for singing. It seems impossible to find an answer to this. Acoustics are good for one or the other, but never both.

When we returned later that evening Valerie was there to greet us, looking lovely and also pleased, as well she might, since her efforts had raised many thousands of pounds for a good cause.

The foyer was filled with elegantly gowned and bejewelled women. A Charity gala may not be the performer's favourite audience but it is certainly the best to look at. When I went out onto the platform I was confronted by the splendour of Merchant Taylors' glorious wood panelling, equally wonderful acoustics, the sight of billowing evening dresses, and the sweet face of the Duchess of Kent in the front row. There was quite a bit of hanging around to do but a lot of beautiful rooms to wander about in. I thought of my early morning call the following day, as I am due to attend a production rehearsal on *Mary Stuart* from 10.30 a.m., and hoped we would be home before midnight. We were!

Thursday 18 March English National Opera has bought the old Decca recording studios, just around the corner from West Hampstead tube station. It is a very easy journey for me; I take the big Metropolitan line from Harrow Hill, change into the little train at Wembley Park and pootle gently down the line. It took twenty-five minutes from door to door, so I was early.

We rehearsed in what used to be studio 3 where, years and years ago, aged twenty-two, I sat on the stepped platforms at one end, as a member of the Ambrosian Singers; thrilled to bits to be recording some Gilbert and Sullivan (I think). I watched Elsie Morrison, Jennifer Vyvyan and Richard Lewis being put through their paces and thought they looked pretty ancient. They must have been all of forty at the time! It's a funny thing how 'old' recedes further and further into the distance the closer one approaches it! Today, even longer in the tooth myself, I wonder what the youngsters in our choirs think of me: 'Poor thing – she's still staggering on!'

I have beloved John Copley again and the production came to me quickly. Certain aspects of the character seem to put themselves forward as we do this piece for the third time. Mary's vulnerability, for instance. Historically, Donizetti has imagined the central scene of the opera when he makes the two Queens

117

meet face to face. It is a really wonderful piece of theatre and knowing what a typical woman Elizabeth I was in so many ways – her feminine pre-occupation with her looks and her clothes, for instance – I wouldn't be a bit surprised if she peeped through the hole in some panelling out of sheer curiosity, to see what this cousin of hers really looked like! The opera is viewed through the eyes of an Italian Roman Catholic, Donizetti, and is biased in every way towards Mary. Knowing the historic facts, it is necessary for me to ignore them and look at the situation from the opposite point of view from the one usually taught in schools. The only way it can work is if I believe utterly that *I* am the rightful Queen of England and that Elizabeth is the usurper and a bastard into the bargain. Immediately Mary's so called 'treason' is then changed into patriotism, and her years of plotting and scheming the natural behaviour of someone who believes the throne of England truly belongs to her. The opera is about her imprisonment both as a young girl when she is still full of hope, and sixteen years later when bitterness has wrapped itself around her character. She is wonderful to play and totally believable in her actions. How many of us could inspire a large group of devoted friends to share years of imprisonment? Mary must have had the most extra-ordinary personality and magnetism to keep such friends and in those conditions. What a period in history to contain two such women for so many years in the same country.

It really is Spring today; the light is strong until 6.30.

Friday 19 March As I have joined the cast late, having had other engagements to fulfil, the first orchestra rehearsal came today after only one day on production. As always, the opera begins to come so vividly alive as soon as one hears the full score, and it is thrilling to sit in front of the curtain singing out to an empty house, just concentrating on the score.

It is a strange but very nice coincidence that two of my last three operas should be with Sir Charles Mackerras and John Copley. We have done some exciting productions together in this house. The atmosphere is different from Covent Garden, altogether more homely, somehow, and less intimidating in a way.

Charles could see I was enjoying myself enormously up there this morning, and my delight in the clearly defined and contrasting rhythms of the Donizetti score immediately transferred itself to him across the pit. I could see his shoulders and body react to my voice as he caught my mood and responded to it in his own inimitable way. These private moments in the making of music are very dear to me. The job is total joy – no audience, just a group of colleagues getting on with the work, with nothing in the way of performers and score.

A very quick lunch, then by train to the rehearsal studios and a long hard afternoon with the chorus until 6.15 p.m. The splendid John Tomlinson is playing Talbot again, magnificently; David Rendall in fine form is Leicester, and Alan Opie is Cecil. He is ideal for the role and scares me to death which is exactly what he should do! The first performances of Elizabeth were given by Pauline Tinsley, and memorable they were too. She looked exactly like the portraits, it was quite uncanny, and we were excellent foils for each other. The second run was with Ava June, a very different interpretation from a beautiful singer.

Now I have an exciting young new star, Rosalind Plowright, who has a thrilling voice and presence. She is taller than I am, which contradicts history again, because Mary was six feet tall and towered above most women. Rosalind is wearing flat pumps and I am wearing high heels!

Sunday My mother's sister Elsie is staying with us for a brief holiday.
21 March My heart turns over when I look at her, the resemblance is quite

Rehearsing *Mary Stuart*   With Rosalind Plowright

obvious and out of a family of eight brothers and sisters, the two kept close contact all their lives. My aunt, the wife of a miner, has spent her entire life in a South Yorkshire mining village and what family I have consists of the aunts, uncles, cousins and second cousins who still live there. They are hard working people; parents and children devoted to each other (it is rare for the younger generation to move far away from parents), with tremendous humour of the ripe Yorkshire kind, and running through the family sharp intelligence and vocal ability, which I believe first made its appearance with my maternal grandparents. My father's parents, who lived in a village about seven miles away, were also admirable, disciplined, hard-working respectable people; my grandfather was groom, then later chauffeur, to the local squire. I always thought them very 'rich' when I was a child, because they not only owned their own house with a lovely garden but also had a car. My grandparents had collected rather beautiful things, one or two nice pieces of furniture, ornaments and books; I have some of them still. During the 1939–1945 war, travel was not encouraged and my horizons stretched from York, via a two hour bus ride, to Doncaster, where in one direction my grandmother lived and in another my Auntie Elsie; we divided our visits between the two. My grandmother's house fascinated me. I would wander through the rooms looking at the most amazing treasures; a brass cobra, photograph frames made of blue bead work, tea caddies in dark, polished wood, and most delightful of all – an American organ with pedals which one had to work with the feet in order to pump air into the instrument. I used to sit there furiously pedalling away playing tremendous pieces, years before I learned music on the piano. I made the most awful row but everyone put up with it without grumbling; they must have felt like murdering me!

Running up the path into the waiting arms of my aunt is the earliest memory I have of her. She would sweep me up and hug me tight, laughing with pleasure. I no longer run to her, she no longer lifts me! But the feeling is exactly the same, her pleasure at seeing me makes me feel as I did when I was a little girl, that here is someone who loves without reserve.

For a long time, my background and my working world created a battleground in me. Most of the performers I know well seem to come, as I do, from ordinary families. I have come to understand that this is exactly how it should be – at least in my own case. I no longer fight the alien attitude which causes me to feel a bit of an outsider when I am with the family group on occasions like weddings, for instance. Last year my second cousin, Janice, who is also my god-daughter, was married and we all got together for this lovely occasion. It was an extremely interesting experience to be surrounded by the faces which not only reminded me of my mother but most strongly of myself! They all treat me with a deeply touching mixture of affection, pride and respect, and that particular day brought home to me how much I owe to the genes which come from them, and to the sanity and stability I inherit from my parents, qualities for which the other world I inhabit brings out an urgent need. If I were really to believe the things people say to me, both good and bad, to imagine that I actually 'belong' in the situations to which my job takes me, from Buckingham Palace downwards, I should be a rather pitiful person. But the years have taught me that the part of me which is a down-to-earth, Yorkshire working woman and the part of me which is an artist, can live together peaceably and enjoy all the different facets of this extra-ordinary life of mine; the battle has ceased to rage; I do have a foot in both worlds and somehow I have managed a balancing act, emerging with a deep gratitude for my roots, and my art. There are indeed many diverse pieces of the jig-saw puzzle but I am beginning to see that they can fit into a pattern, and make up a coherent whole rather than tear me apart, making me feel as though I don't truly belong anywhere. I am a fortunate person, not least in my loving parents who, without knowing the slightest thing about the musical profession, nevertheless gave me every support, moral and financial; my profession has treated me kindly; I still have the ideals, the reverence and joy in great music with which I started out. My father sums it all up though; he says of artists, 'You're all barmy but you're not quite so barmy as some!'

Monday
22 March Here's a strange start to the week! I am in Bond Street at the Autumn Show of my favourite *couturier*, Murray Arbeid, to whom I was introduced by a friend in Edinburgh. Murray is really a wholesaler but he does make a few things for a small number of clients, and luckily I am one. He has a tremendous sense of the dramatic which is so important in the concert hall; he uses big shapes, singing colours and superb cut, all of which show to great advantage in large spaces. I have enjoyed most of the dresses I've worn over the years and am very fond of the soft, fluid shapes which Yuki has made for me but I wanted a complete change of style. The gowns Murray has devised are the best for my particular requirements and are wonderful to wear. I was very nervous the first time I attended one of his shows. He wanted me to see the collection on the models, since looking at garments on hangers is simply not the same. He is quite right. A show is a thing of joy and beauty, especially on a Monday morning. I have to be in my seat by 9.45 a.m.! But it is worth getting up early for. Today the fabrics and the colours are marvellous and I shall have difficulty making a choice. All the good designers have a 'signature', which is immediately recognisable when you have seen a bit of their work. The evening dress is Murray's particular genius although I saw some day clothes this morning which I would love. I always imagined the buyers, who sit there with pencils poised, writing and drawing, would be the most svelte, glamorous, well-dressed people imaginable. They aren't!

123

A smart move over to West Hampstead where I begin my morning reheasal at 11.15.

It is a truly glorious Spring day, a cloudless sky. Good to be alive and healthy enough to enjoy it.

Tuesday 23 March   Into the theatre for the first time. Re-doing this production is rather like a tremendously speeded-up film; *Alceste* would therefore be in slow motion; every bar of every scene painstakingly rehearsed over and over again. *Mary Stuart* is such familiar ground that a different problem emerges – how not to get stale – how to preserve a certain freshness of the character. Curiously, I find I am singing 'her' more easily than ever before. I put this down to the fact that I am better at pacing the scenes, there are certain moments where I can conserve emotional energy. Donizetti has helped a great deal because his thoughtful planning of the role enables the singers to have these moments of gentleness before launching out once more into the intense dramatic pieces. Of course, any kind of singing is tremendously hard work for the body but to learn when one can keep something in reserve is invaluable.

Saturday 27 March   Our first Dress Rehearsal, with piano, but we have to be in the theatre by 9.30 to get make-up and wigs on too. These rehearsals are valuable because I can do a certain amount of experimenting with the make-up base which, because I am blonde in my first scene, grey in the second and auburn in the last, creates difficulties in choosing a basic colour to suit each wig; once the face is done I can't change it as there isn't enough time in between acts. By the end of a long morning we had the new black velvet sorted out, it has a tricky collar and John wasn't absolutely satisfied about the skirt until Bill had a brain-wave, did something technical, and went down on his bended knees to persuade me to try it on again before I left for home! I was happy to do so, since I myself had been bolshie, first about my poor dresser who came in with a streaming cold and had hardly got her head round the door before I sent her away again, and then about my new shoes which were to make me taller than Rosalind. I put them on, marched around the dressing room feeling like a Frankenstein monster, took them off and put on my old ones, deciding to hit my paranoia about being smaller than my Elizabeth firmly on the head! Comfort first. The third act cloak which has caused me such distress, is now so light and comfortable I could wear it all day. John said, 'You're crazy – why didn't you ask us to do something about it before?' Don't know the answer to that!

Another heavenly day and the clocks go forward. Then early bed because of tomorrow.

Sunday
28 March
St. Matthew Day! Up at nine to be made-up, dressed, well warmed up, and at the Festival Hall by 11 a.m. Our annual pilgrimage. Often, this English performance with the Bach Choir is the only one I do in the year but today I have the wonderful memory of King's still ringing in my ears. This one is different in so many ways. It is achingly familiar; the whole tradition of the early rising, the picnic in my dressing room in between the two parts, the sense of dedicated enjoyment generated by this special audience (many of them come every single year); this famous choir with its long dignified tradition, my own collaboration with them, and with Sir David Willcocks, their conductor, which now goes back so many years, all adds up to an atmosphere just as unique in its way for me as the King's performance. The Festival Hall, dear and familiar though it is, cannot be the ideal place for Bach; I miss the feeling of a church so

125

much: the memories of performances in St. Bartholomew's with the London Bach Society and Dr. Paul Steinitz are particularly dear to me. But as the performance extends into the afternoon, the concentration and the sharing of this Mount Everest of all musical experiences rises above every consideration, and the only thing that matters is the life-enhancing unfolding of the Passion story told by the greatest master of them all, Bach, and our chance, performers and audience alike, to share in this wonder and be *changed* by it. I measure a year's life on this day. Involvement in this piece forces me to ask questions of myself; what was my feeling last year compared with today? What have I learned about myself during these twelve months? How have I changed, if at all? Have I developed as a musician? The only honest answer I can give myself is to admit that there has *been* change. Whether for 'good' or 'bad' no longer concerns me. I am grateful for the fact that I am not standing in the same place. Certain things have altered; some things are quite obvious to me, such as the increasing feeling of peace and stability; I am beginning to look at myself with much more compassion after having driven myself relentlessly for a quarter of a century; perhaps this too was necessary and not to be regretted. Is it middle age which teaches us to put a gentle, kindly veil over what we are, and in becoming kinder to ourselves, therefore kinder to other people? Is this what that impossible command to *Love our neighbour as ourselves* may mean? I just hope there may never come a day when I can sit through this Passion music untouched by the experience, or unchanged by the passage of time.

As music at its greatest is for me an experience of the fourth dimension, that is, all human experience plus the extra one of *time*, past present and future, so is the Passion the truest single reflection of music as a whole, because it gathers up every factor, composer, music, performer, audience, and while leaving us complete individuals binds us together as one. If this is not an expression of Holiness, I don't know what is.

126

Monday
29 March It was 9 p.m. as we drove away from the theatre after a difficult and frustrating day. Although we were made up, bewigged and costumed from 2 p.m. the rehearsal was really for Charles and the orchestra and this meant stopping every few bars to correct, then repeat, a phrase. Charles is most anxious that the playing will be of the highest possible quality since this production is being preserved both by recording and video tape. Quite understandable, but it has driven us crazy. We would launch into a move with gusto and be arrested in the middle of it feeling foolish! Eventually we saw the funny side and made the best of it. The long hours passed. My second act dress and cap are still undergoing minor changes; John Copley isn't yet absolutely satisfied. Everyone took bits and pieces of me away and worked quietly in corners, snipping, re-shaping, compromising. It will be alright tomorrow for the Dress Rehearsal. As we must be in by 9.30 a.m. I wondered whether it would be a good idea to sink peacefully down onto our dressing room floors and sleep there. No-one seemed to agree!

Tuesday
30 March 'Up betimes', as the famous diarist said. On the station platform trying to hide myself behind dark glasses, hoping not to see anyone I know. I do, of course, precisely that, but it is a young friend of ours, a neighbour's daughter, who makes no attempt to scurry away down the platform but appears to want to travel into town with me. We have what I think is a pleasant, easy conversation which makes me happy. It is such a wonder to me when other people's children actually talk to me and tell me about their doings; Katharine is at Cambridge and with brains, looks, and a 21st birthday party in the offing, is quite radiant. It is a great beginning to the day. Young people of all ages are a treat for Keith and me. They breeze briefly in and out of our house and lives and we see the best of them. Parents with all the responsibility, heart-ache and joy have a very different

127

experience; childless couples are alighted upon for a brief moment like plants by butterflies, and then left, but with a sense of something sweet and touching.

Today the theatre was packed with people. How to give enough, but not too much, leaving something in reserve for Thursday – that's the difficulty. There were many moments when I simply could not hold back; this opera is so incredibly involving. The deep emotions which one has to find for great characterisation take an energy which comes from somewhere so deep within, one feels like a vacuum afterwards. Alceste was grief-stricken from beginning to end. So is Orfeo, but a manly grief will be different to play. Mary Stuart comes running on to the stage like a teenager, and in the first twenty minutes of the second act depicts ecstatic joy, fear, despair, terrible anger, and suicidal defiance. She later has to show the bitter iron of imprisonment, stark terror at the news of her beheading, hidden from Cecil but poured out upon her jailer Talbot. She goes through a soul-searching confession, then calm and undaunted takes leave of her friends, prays with them, forgives Elizabeth, absolves the English from 'the scourge of the Lord', and finally walks blindfold to the scaffold! And I wonder why I am tired!

I crawled into bed and slept, without even bathing first. Here I am again, in exactly the same situation as at the end of the arduous *Alceste* rehearsals, so bone-weary I can't speak. I feel like one of those metal wire sculptures which quiver all over when you pass a hand over them. If anyone passed a hand over me all my nerve endings would scream!

I think one of the problems of performing is being a middle-man. I was describing my feelings of having a foot in two worlds; well, artistically I see I also straddle two worlds: a performer is a bridge between the creative genius and the audience. The divine fire which feeds creativity also nourishes the creative person and he needs it because his is the most difficult job. Re-creative people are one remove from the fire; we receive it by reflection through the actual work, the piece of music or the play, but at the same time we are pulled in two directions both of which take energy from us – responsibility to the composer and then to the audience.

This 'energy leak' is another way of describing dedication. The artist has to be as selfless as possible, like a medium in a seance; the medium is used *by* something *for* something else, and when the person wakes from the trance, so one is told, he or she suffers a form of depletion and can only repeat the process after time has elapsed. Now singers are all different in terms of the amount of time necessary to gain back enough strength to perform again. It is one of the hardest lessons and one of the most important ones a young person has to learn – exactly how much can be done, how often. I find as I am growing older that I need more and more recovery time and it is precisely in the area of the theatre where I don't get it. Between Monday and Thursday this week I shall have completed three full-scale performances, only one of which is the 'real' one. Next week, instead of a good long break, we have to do hours of rehearsal so that the camera-men can learn our moves for the video-taping. It is this kind of pressure that I no longer wish to subject myself to.

130

Neither can I go on producing the immense range of emotional colour this character, or any character for that matter, rightly demands. Acting is, like the written word, a sacred thing; I can't skim the surface. I am totally involved; there are many levels of playing, you can see them all around you as you stand on a stage, but acting is too important to 'play-act'. For me, it is all or nothing.

Wednesday
31 March 'Are you religious?' This question, flung towards me like a bucket of ice-cold water, has cropped up in almost every interview I've ever given. I want to yell back, 'But what do you *mean* by "religious"?' I usually reply quietly, 'I am a communicant member of the Church of England,' which seems to satisfy most journalists.

But as I am recording this year of my life I can't do so without mentioning the Something or Somebody which I believe sustains me at every moment of every day. What I shall try to describe is the most sacred and private aspect of a person's life – the relationship he has with his God.

The influence on my development which stands on equal terms with the musical one has been through reading. On countless occasions I have put down a book and given heartfelt thanks to the author for having shared something with me, and in the sharing helped me to broaden my understanding. There are no words for the kind of gratitude one feels for another who, in revealing the soul, holds out a hand in the darkness to someone unknown. My debt is enormous to such people, and this is my own attempt to put the indescribable into feeble words, just in case someone, somewhere, can relate to it.

I know a number of truly wonderful 'Christians' who never set foot inside a church, but I was brought up to attend church regularly and I am deeply grateful to my parents who established

this pattern for me. Now, nearly fifty years old, I still need the 'Faith of my fathers' to the extent that I try to go to our beautiful little church of St. Mary's whenever I can. I want to worship in a consecrated building and I want to take the sacraments, not because I think I am any better than those who don't (I know I am not), but because I need all the help I can get!

Years ago, not very well off, living alone in a tiny bed-sitter which contained a bed, a chair, a table, a piano and a telephone (I thought I was in clover!), my visits home were the highlights of my life; but getting back on the train to London, having said goodbye to my mother and father, was practically impossible, made so by the pain of my separation from them and the loneliness of my existence at the other end. I would sit in the train, unable even to read, fighting back the tears and the anguish of homesickness; I used to call, silently, on the name of Jesus to help me. I was in this situation only because I honestly believed He had given me work to do as a singer. For no other reason would I have ever stuck my first four years as a student. Well, Jesus didn't actually come and sit beside me in the railway carriage, at least, I don't think so, but I *was* given the courage to carry on with my training. I could make a simple cry for help because of the way in which I had been brought up; that tradition forms the bottom layer of the cake, as it were; I take the facts of Christianity as the foundation. At first, they were all I had, or needed. Then I began to read, widely, books on comparative religions, psychology, in particular Carl Jung, philosophy, the lives of mystics of many denominations; that huge world of ideas and experience fed me and has continued to do so. To be plunged into this world can prove disastrous to a simple faith; my experience has been a series of forays into new territory, always returning to base but with a richer understanding of it, and the ability to see that what I learned elsewhere was actually right there in my own religion all the time, rather like the situation when parents tell their children certain things for

133

years to no effect. Then along comes an outsider, saying exactly the same, and enlightenment strikes!

For many years this 'journey' of mine into the minds of others was a lonely one. There are relatively few people who want to explore this particular world. Then, quite recently, I found myself included in the lives of three like-minded people; the occasions when we meet and talk are precious to me. Through them, in the curious ways such things seem to work, I met a remarkable woman, a Sufi and a saint, who wrote a book which I read with great interest; the actual impact of her personality was another turning-point for me. A group meets regularly to meditate at her house, and she agreed to let me join it whenever I could. She told me later that she was reluctant to do so at first, because the arrival of a 'famous' person could easily have caused some disruption. This has not proved the case. When I am free, I creep in, sit on the floor (we meditate in silence), sometimes leaving immediately afterwards if I have to, sometimes staying on a little to talk to the others. They all accept me as a private person; many of them don't know who I am anyway, those who do, respect my desire to be just a member of the group and for this I am infinitely grateful. Meditation does not intrude in any way upon the different religions of those who meet there; I have found, as I do with my reading, that it enriches and deepens Christianity for me.

The layers of the cake then, begin with my childhood faith, continue with the influence of many different kinds of thought, then my friends of other persuasions, and the all-important contact with a human being of great holiness, who, I believe in some way transfers a sort of grace to those who visit her.

This adds up to a paradox. I was taught to believe and I still do believe that there is only one religion – the Christian religion; it *is* the only one for me. But I also accept the evidence of my own eyes in seeing the actions and the quality of life of people who do not believe as I do, or who may not believe in God, as I understand the word, at all; this evidence tells me that there are an infinite number of ways to God and that I have no right to judge the state of anybody's soul. I have a great deal to learn from such people.

Ultimately, 'religion' means one simple thing; it is the relationship an individual has with his Maker. It is a one-to-one affair. I have come to the conclusion that at all the crisis times, one is utterly alone. When I am singing, regardless of those who taught me, those who have worked with me on a piece of music, regardless of the musicians surrounding me, I am absolutely alone. There is no-one to get me through the final moment of opening my mouth and doing it, except myself – myself and One Other; at times of great distress, suffering or bereavement, I have felt exactly the same. Alone, but alone with God. There is no security in the world or in people, however much we love them. No-one can actually see inside another's heart and mind; we all presume, and sometimes quite successfully, that we can share each other's joys and sorrows; in a certain way we do. But the miracle of belief is that our inevitable alone-ness reveals Someone else; that Someone else is, if you like, 'inside us' – closer than that. He knows everything about us, everything we say and do and are. And knowing all this, loves us without reservation.

The Creator has made the Universe, dwells in it, and at the same time dwells in us. If we allow Him to live our life, He will make us feel a secure, loved and precious part of His creation. To approach this security, this Love, and to feel it, even in the smallest way, is the life task of every one of us. The approach entails the knowing of what we are – in order to know That which Is, and it means death – the death of our illusions about ourselves. It is the hardest task we will ever undertake and it is the only one worth struggling to complete. Perhaps it is easy to say all this enjoying a wonderful, satisfying life, well fed, healthy, surrounded by a loving family and good friends. I hope I would say it in other

135

circumstances, but I can only state my terms within the framework of the life I have been given.

No-one can prove that Creation 'means' anything. The terror, the destruction, which occurs in Nature is enough to turn many people away from the idea of a loving Father completely. The problems of suffering, pain, and evil surround us, for which explanation may never be given; nevertheless, I choose to believe that behind it all is a sense of order, of purpose, and finally of Love, because I could not live with the despair a hopeless Universe would awaken in me. We all desperately need something which will not fail us. The idea of God and the living reality of a loving Father is the centre which sustains me, giving me the possiblity to feel loved – loved unfailingly – in spite of what I am; the possibility to live without judging myself and therefore without judging others; to realise that if God can love me as I am, it is possible for me to love others just as *they* are. I do not claim for one moment that my small understanding has made me 'better'. It has not. But it is changing the way I look at the world and at people.

Thursday   Usual habits of performance day: get up to shop for cards and
1 April   one or two presents for the cast, practise in my music room – without piano. The innards of my Bechstein have gone away to Samuels for an overhaul. My lungs are in a bolshevik mood; tired of all the deep breathing required of them, they send a message to my brain as I begin my exercises: 'Not again! Why can't you leave us alone?' Objection over-ruled. First period of warming-up over, I return to bed with a bowl of cereals – all the good ones, bran, wheat-germ, muesli, etc. – and eat them before settling down in the hope that I shall sleep. I do, for two lovely hours. I then get up to practise again; the old engine is now running nicely. Keith brings me my dinner (5 p.m.!) of steak, salad, and a pear, glass of milk to follow, with a ginger biscuit as a

136

treat to finish off with. I pin up my hair, get dressed, pack my bag, and we are off by 5.45. My father looks smart in his bow tie and dark suit, so does Keith.

Hardly any traffic, we are at Marble Arch in twenty minutes. The London traffic is unpredictable these days.

My boys go off to park the car and I try to get into my dressing room which is already so packed with flowers I can hardly squeeze in. Gillian, my dresser, finds a huge bucket, fills it with water, and we put them into it, so the bouquets will not hang around for hours in a hot room, wilting. Can't bear that. They are so beautiful and standing in my bathroom fill the whole area with marvellous scent. Lots of kind messages to read, then I put my cards around me, set my table, and begin the job of make-up. It goes well tonight, clean lines, good foundation. My hand does not shake as I do the tricky area around the eyes. I am pleased with it.

I have plenty of time because I am not in the first act at all. Charles comes in. I have been anxious to see him because he had given me a working tape of the Dress Rehearsal which the recording company took to experiment for balance. It has been absolutely invaluable and I learned a great deal from listening to it, even at this early stage. I want to discuss with Charles the things he wishes to change. We have the most valuable, stimulating, and fascinating ten minutes of communicative, co-operative conversation. It is such a good feeling when minds meet and agree as ours do. Even when we don't agree, we can always find a working compromise. I owe so much to this man, who has encouraged me to explore an ever wider range of styles and roles. The best conductors are hell-bent on achieving the best results; they do this in a totally impersonal way. They are not concerned with individuals in the normal sense. The individual is always part of a much more important whole, which must be an extremely difficult task to weld together, bearing in mind every person, every musician, involved in an opera; but

137

Charles makes me feel like a valued ally, sharing in his enormous task. I certainly do share in his determination to find, somehow, the best possible all-round performance. It is wonderful when a conductor treats you as a respected equal rather than an unintelligent cog-in-the-wheel, which is the way singers are often thought of.

Curtain up. The audience sounds absolutely with us tonight, at least through the tannoy. Rosalind is in her greatest form and having the triumph she deserves.

Curtain up on Act II and I am on. That first run is scary – I always wonder if I will slip! Tonight I don't, and as Mary turns and twists in the joy of finding herself in the open air, let out of her prison for exercise at long last, I feel something of the joy she must have felt.

In what seems like two minutes the act is over and I am back in my dressing room, shattered, deeply shaken and exhausted by all the tremendous emotional changes I've had to portray in the last thirty-five minutes. Keith comes in very red around the eyes.

Rehearsal and performance (i) With David Rendall, Act II

Rehearsal and performance (ii) With Rosalind Plowright, Act II

Rehearsal and performance (iii) With David Rendall and John Tomlinson, Act II

Rehearsal and performance (iv) With John Tomlinson, Act III

He is shattered too and can't speak, obviously much moved by the whole thing, but doesn't stay long.

Dressed for Act III. The door opens quietly and Peter Moores comes in. He is the generous and philanthropic person who has made the recording possible. He tells me he is sitting in the recording room and asks me if I am pleased. I reply that such a question is impossible to answer but that I am enjoying myself. I shall be interested to hear the new batch of tapes at the weekend after which another session of discussion with Charles will take place.

I go on for Act III, a piece of colossal and extended singing with no let-up whatsoever except a brief costume change. It is vital that I pace it correctly and have enough vocal, physical and spiritual energy to make the final singing as exciting and spine-chilling as it should be. Tonight, thanks to our conversation and the way Charles catches, encourages, and shapes my every phrase down there in the pit, I think we achieve something memorable.

Curtain down, hugs all round, and a visit from Princess Alexandra, looking slender, elegant and beautiful. Her facial bone structure I would give my soul for! She is easy, friendly, and sweet to us.

Then visitors, and clean up, and I am ready for our small supper party at L'Opera where we have a superb meal and a relaxing time with Charles, his darling wife Judy, and a few other friends.

Home and into bed by 2 a.m.

Friday 2 April These are the simple chronological facts of yesterday. They do not and cannot describe the amount of work, the loss of life-energy, a singer gives out in order to make a score and a character come alive. I popped into Rosalind's dressing room just before she went on stage for her first scene, and I took her

142

hands in mine. They were ice-cold, like the hands of a dead person. I could see in her eyes exactly what she was going through and as I went back into my room my own eyes were full of tears because I knew what she was feeling. Only another performer can ever fully understand what a performer suffers in order to give to other people. My sympathy for my young colleague, at the outset of what I am sure will be a great career, was total. She has many years of moments like that in front of her. Somehow she will deal with them as I have done, as we all do.

The house is quiet, the sun is shining outside, it will soon be Easter, and this evening I shall go to a little house in North London, sit down on the floor and meditate in silence with a group of friends.

Saturday My colleague Josephine Veasey has given her last performance at
3 April Covent Garden – a dignified, quiet withdrawal, commanding the sort of respect and admiration which has been a hall-mark of her long, faithful service to the Opera House; it must be thirty years at least. The circus which surrounds my own operatic appearances this year, however, does have two distinctly positive aspects. The first is of determination that my real 'goodbye', when it happens, will be equally private; the second is the impetus it has given me to attempt this task of synthesizing the current year, putting thoughts into words, focussing the mind to clarify. It is as much a voyage of discovery for me as a description of my reflections each day. I have, on occasion, the strongest impulse to put the entire manuscript into the waste-paper basket, feeling revolted by the further exposure publication will bring. But if I don't write about myself, one of the many hounds baying at the door certainly will.

I return again and again to the question of fatigue. My reader will think I spend most of my free time flat out from exhaustion!

Fischer-Dieskau says a singer has two positions – standing up and lying down! It is impossible to explain to anyone who doesn't sing the physical stress on the body but it is an inescapable fact which, of course, we endeavour to hide during performance. There are very few jobs which entail such depletion of mental, physical, and spiritual reserves as this one. The other side of the coin is complete fulfilment while one is doing it. I do not have children. I do have, or have had in previous years, all sorts of advice from strangers impertinent enough to give it, as to why I *should* have them. Can I claim, as a woman, to feel completely fulfilled? There are innumerable ways for human beings to 'give birth'. You do not have to be female but you do have to be a channel for life. That is precisely what re-creative people are; we conduct life force through the vehicle of music. It does not always happen, but on many occasions, as I know from wonderful letters I receive or from the face of someone who comes to a Green Room to say a simple but heartfelt 'Thank you', our work can give birth to change, can touch, heal, comfort, or bring joy to the human heart. This power is not ours; it is the extra ingredient which descends during those moments when the performer is in the correct frame of mind, willing to be used by something greater than he is. This power is not a prerogative of artists; anyone can discover it in any simple act made by one person to another in the course of daily life; a kindly word, a small act of unselfishness, a smile, a visit to a lonely person. Artists are wielding this power at any one moment to large numbers of people. In ordinary life the numbers are smaller, but the process is exactly the same, and so is the end result – fulfilment. I would suggest that when a performance (as to some extent all performances do) reveals this mysterious 'power', the way it is received shows nothing more or less than the state of mind and heart of the person at the receiving end. How the individual feels about it should tell him a great deal about himself.

144

Sunday
4 April
A beautiful Spring morning. I wanted to canter round the garden like a Whitbread dray horse on its annual holiday. I once saw a film of them let out to graze and will never forget the sight of their great bodies, and their unmistakable joy as they ran about the field.

It is easy to understand what a hold Spring had on the imagination of people who practised pagan rites of welcome to it at this time of year. We spent hours outside and did some useful work; we did *not* canter or dance naked around the lawns; went quietly to St. Mary's for Evensong instead.

Monday
5 April
Into the theatre early to start rehearsing all over again for the TV cameras, feeling a great reluctance to begin at the beginning, or almost, when we have already done a first night.

The lights on stage are now much brighter and to my astonishment the stalls are full of contraptions; the cameras are quite visible and I suppose the paying public will be placed on the higher levels.

We all wore our big practice skirts; the long morning wore on with constant stops and starts. The rest of the cast, which worked all day yesterday too, was exhausted. 'My' camera team was also in the theatre today, filming us being filmed, so to speak!

Tuesday
6 April
My father's seventy-seventh birthday. I am deeply grateful he is so well and able to lead an independent life, even though we are all under the same roof. For an elderly person to have his own flat and cook his meals is important for the sense of dignified wellbeing it brings. Long may it last.

Dress Rehearsal this morning. I enjoy sitting in my dressing room while someone else does the make-up; there is something very relaxing about having one's face done. The finished job,

145

With my father

which took about an hour, was vastly different from the one I usually do for stage work myself, altogether paler and softer. Out we went for Act II, and at the end of it my face had to be done all over again because the extra lights had drained the colours. Studio lighting is different and the make-up would have been fine under those circumstances. When the girls saw us on the monitors they knew immediately that they would have to deepen the colouring. Second time round I looked as I usually do for the stage.

Three enormous vans from the television centre are parked outside the stage door, blocking up the narrow street. The theatre staff are excited by this intrusion of another world – it changes the atmosphere in the theatre, blowing like a fresh wind through the building.

Although yesterday we were all acutely conscious of the camera positions and the red lights going off and coming on again, today we went through the opera without concerning ourselves unduly about them. We are anxious to preserve energy for the actual performance tomorrow.

<table>
<tr><td>Wednesday
7 April</td><td>There was a definite air of anticipation backstage tonight; the audience was affected too, the atmosphere in the theatre was electric. This, in turn, set the scene for what followed, and I believe what we got onto tape was a most exciting performance, beautifully paced by Charles who was enjoying himself in the pit as much as we were on stage. The production was hardly altered at all for the cameras; in one or two places we were asked to stand closer together, and because of this the moment when Mary and Elizabeth meet for the first time was actually strengthened, since the eye contact was at a distance of three feet and created a powerful tension. I hope to keep this change in. The heat generated by the extra lights which had been installed was colossal and I was dripping with perspiration all night long.</td></tr>
</table>

There were no retakes to do and afterwards everybody met upstairs for a meal and congratulations all round.

As Keith and I walked across the stage to the front of house the entire area was open, the side cloths had been removed and the backstage area seemed one with the auditorium – a huge open space – filled with men hard at work taking the set to pieces. It hit me suddenly that I had only four more performances in this friendly theatre. I watched for my next reaction – would it be a sickening sense of regret or pain? All I felt was a tremendous joy at the thought of the evening just completed and gratitude for my memories of the Coliseum and what it has given me.

<table>
<tr><td>Thursday
8 April</td><td>The day after is rather like being an invalid. I can stay in bed, I can feel tired, lazy, not talking to anyone, all without the slightest sense of guilt!</td></tr>
</table>

147

The first thing is to get really clean. Theatre make-up is clogging to the pores and my hair is a terrible sight after being squashed under wigs. Pristine from top to toe, I can then tackle my new batch of 'thank-you's' for the lovely flowers I was given last night.

Then a little work on my manuscript which must be kept absolutely up to date. As I write, the sections are sent off to the publisher for editing, sent back to me, then returned; we are working to an extremely tight deadline and everyone involved in the production of my book is alerted and prepared for this unusual method. The last pages, hot from my pen after the final night of *Orfeo* at Glyndebourne, will be rushed to the printer, after correction, to meet publication date at the end of October. To me, an absolute novice, the whole operation is a miracle of planning and organisation, and as each stage is handed to me to see, the possibility that at the end of the process a book will emerge grows stronger. As with record sleeves, over which, sadly, I have no control whatsoever, the jacket design, now ready, is of paramount importance and I have been allowed to approve it; no difficulty there at all; we narrowed the suggestions down to two, and the final choice is everything I could wish for and more.

I have been given John Mortimer's autobiography *Clinging to the Wreckage* as an Easter egg, and settled down this afternoon for a good long read. The rest of us might just as well pack it in and shut up shop. I sat and laughed like a lunatic all afternoon. To make people laugh! What a thing. I wonder if naturally funny people enjoy themselves as much as we enjoy them? Oh! Mr Mortimer, you've made my day.

Friday
9 April Easter: the first holiday of the year has the quality of an opera when one considers the high drama of Act I, Good Friday: the appearance of our church, bereft of colour, the altar cross hidden

148

underneath a linen cover, the heaviness of those hours from 12 noon to 3 p.m. I feel such a sense of relief when they are over for another year. The only other day which has this same feeling for me is Remembrance Sunday. I want to run away and hide until it's over. The days of Passion Week, starting with Palm Sunday, contain extraordinary elements of theatre; for people in mediaeval times who relied totally on church pageantry to bring colour into their lives the events must have been overwhelming.

Saturday 10 April Easter Saturday, a performance day. I feel there is no contradiction at all in going to work during this holy time. It seems so right that as an entertainer it is my job to do precisely that for those of the population who are enjoying the first break of the year, particularly when I am playing a character to whom religion meant everything. Act II, Easter Saturday, has all the elements a middle act should have; a sense of relaxation because one can't keep up the same tension all the time, and of anticipation – the church has been decked out in its very best clothes and is full of flowers. Then finally, tomorrow, the splendour, joy and glory of Act III, Easter Day, and all it means, to believers in terms of a Resurrection, to Nature bursting with new life, and to the individual who should surely see some signs of change, regeneration, and hope, no matter what his beliefs or circumstances.

Sunday 11 April What a fantastic mixture of everything life is! This weekend has contained all the things which mean most to me – a sense of the Holy, a public performance, and visits from family.

Tuesday 13 April Today I heard the latest batch of tapes, but not at home; I went to the EMI studios and listened to them in the best conditions. From

149

my point of view the second act is safely in the bag. The third act still has quite a long way to go and many good moments were ruined by unguarded coughs; heart-breaking.

Our last chance to achieve the sort of result acceptable for a permanent record. Cecil, Alan Opie, is ill; he was struggling to sing last Saturday in spite of illness, he looked grey underneath his make-up, but has had to succumb completely and Patrick Wheatley took over. This meant none of Cecil's role could be used at all. We are hoping to get permission for the penultimate performance to be taped now, in order to make up for Alan's indisposition. Tonight my own music was satisfactorily completed for the recording, but if we do have to tape again next week, the only performance of the entire run to be free of either TV recording or record taping pressures will be the last one of all.

Before the performance began, the audience and orchestra were asked to give their utmost consideration in stifling coughs and extraneous noise. They all rose marvellously to this endurance test and we hope the result was an unspoiled tape.

I find all the performers growing and developing into their roles as the run progresses. Mary herself shows me new insight into her character each time I play her. Donizetti has kept her changes of mood crystal clear, not only from one scene to the next but from one moment to the next. Leicester tells Mary that Elizabeth has arrived to see her. Immediately she is filled with anxiety, fear, and a reluctance containing elements of dread. The next moment Leicester says, 'But you must show her deference.' The word 'deference' instantly changes Mary's mood into one of utter defiance; she is a Queen again and won't defer to anybody. This new emotion causes a reaction in the body, exactly as it would do in ordinary circumstances. If one listens to what other people are saying, without anticipating by a fraction

150

of a moment, the body will react automatically to the emotion in the mind. It is a hard discipline waiting for the 'trigger' word. Many singers don't do this, and acting is for them a prepared reaction, robbed of its spontaneity and therefore of its reality. The trick is, to refuse to think of the next moment until it actually happens, to sing and to act in that all-important 'Now'. Then everything falls naturally into place and 'acting' comes from the mind first and travels through the body a split second later, not the other way round.

Nothing irritates me more than to feel a colleague with whom I am in close contact begin to push me a second or two before I should actually move away. I know I have to move, but only at the right time! Many people 'work ahead' like this. We must and can trust ourselves absolutely; if the thought is right, the physical reaction is also. If the emotion one is playing is sincerely felt in the heart and mind, the body cannot do anything other than obey; a physical movement or a gesture doesn't need any calculated help from us. A stage is a space where another form of reality is taking place. It is not a place where one 'pretends'. The magical thing about 'acting' is that, just like life, it changes. The 'trigger' word does not induce exactly the same reaction each time. Certain moves become less important on some nights, others more telling. One can never know beforehand which moments will alter; the excitement of trying to hold one's attention in the 'Now' is that the changes do definitely happen; they are the result of the imponderables which surround all performing and bring it alive, not necessarily stemming from the performers themselves, although they often do, but from audiences, or the weather, or a change of cast.

The characters I have played over many years are like people I know very well. I have often been asked how I can possibly play Mary, knowing the historical background. It's easy! Mary saw it all entirely from her own point of view. It is my job to steep myself so deeply into the attitude and state of mind of those I play that I see a score totally from that specific angle. I must succeed to the extent that someone might even say, 'Yes, I can see why she behaved as she did, she could really do no other.' I remember studying Penelope from *The Return of Ulysses* at Glyndebourne with Peter Hall. He had this wonderful idea that she would not want to look at her husband, that somewhere within was this reluctance to face the man who had made her live her life in such a way for twenty years. As I got deeper and deeper into the character of this fabulous woman, I began to understand a little of the resentment, pain, anguish, love and bitter anger she must have felt towards this husband of hers. It seemed to me that her first reaction to his return might well have been to attack him physically for putting her through such agony. Only when she had accepted her mixed emotions completely was she then able to turn and look him in the face. Her own tribulations had been slowly fitting her, shaping her, to make her the woman to whom he was able to return, to make possible her acceptance of him, so that they could start again but on a different level. If nothing had happened to Penelope during all those years, Ulysses would not have found a meeting-ground of compatability, and would probably have left her once more. The revelations such character studies show to the performer are a never-ending delight; it must be just the same for an actor but singers also have the score. We always have this other, fundamental guide, developing, beautifying, deepening the experience for us.

In the last scene of *Mary Stuart* when Cecil offers her the gratification of a final wish, Mary replies, 'First grant me one small favour.' The orchestra, as it plays the harmony underneath 'favour', does something to the word which would never be achieved without the music. Donizetti has imbued that moment with something indescribable, and it is in such moments I feel in full measure just what it is to be a singer.

I was interviewed by Richard Baker in front of an audience of Friends of English National Opera at St. Martin-in-the-Fields. Richard must possess one of the most beautiful speaking voices in the world! He said to me afterwards, 'Answering questions clarifies the mind.' On such occasions many of the questions are familiar, understandably so, and especially the one which inevitably came towards the end of the evening: 'Well, why *are* you retiring from the stage?' I wonder how many times I've heard it in the last few months?

After the interview was over some of us walked to the Coliseum for a short reception. Later, as we left the building to go home, we crossed the stage, an area so familiar to me, a space in which I belong and have a right to be; I realised that after Saturday I should no longer have that right. I thought, if ever I set foot on it again, it will be as a visitor, an outsider, an alien. And it hurt.

It's always the petty, silly irritations which mar a day. This morning began with post, the usual conglomeration of adoring letters, unwanted advice, and abuse. The latter I can tell just by the writing on the envelopes, and usually the first sentence confirms my suspicions; into the waste-paper basket they go! I slept very badly last night, never a good prelude to the following day. The telephone rang incessantly; I looked at the diary for the month of May which we have tried to keep as quiet as possible to give me a breather before Glyndebourne begins; it is an horrific sight, not from the number of engagements but from all the surrounding commitments to people who must positively be seen and attended to before we disappear to the seclusion (I hope!) of Sussex for six weeks.

I dropped yoghurt on my bedroom carpet, having retired for a quiet simple lunch. Keith heard my yell of anguish and thought I had at least fallen out of the bedroom window! The mess was

153

cleared away, and I tried to sleep, unsuccessfully, so I got up and went off to my dentist. I have been plagued with tooth-ache recently in every tooth. The dentist X-rayed my teeth and informed me that for my age (!) they are in excellent condition. He said, 'You are probably grinding your teeth in your sleep. Are you under stress at the moment?' Am I under stress? Well yes, actually life is a bit pressured at the moment, but I thought I had it all fairly under control. I *do* have it under control, but my sub-conscious is peeved by my outer calm, and is obviously taking it out on my teeth. Came home deeply relieved that my teeth are *not* going to drop out one by one in the next five minutes, from some awful disease.

We had tea outside, a relaxed moment, shattered, literally, by my accidentally sweeping cups, saucers, and plates onto the terrace, smashing them in pieces. I looked at Keith, he looked at me. We didn't say a word, but tidied up yet again! I waited for the next calamity. Still very tense as the evening wore on, I said to myself: 'I've had a bad day. I'm at a difficult age, and I can't relax.' I then replied: 'You silly fool, go and sleep it off.' I decided to take my own good advice, and went up to bed.

Wednesday 21 April A whole week since the last performance and a most welcome break. In these glorious Spring days I've tried to prepare myself for next Saturday, which might be a difficult night; I won't know until it actually arrives. Wonderful gardening days! I can't think of any country which is not at its best in the Spring and in the Autumn; most places are either too hot or too cold later on, but at this time of year every climate is in 'balance' before moving on to its extreme.

There is the same beautiful 'balance' in the phases of human life. Just as in Nature, our own Spring, Autumn, and Winter inexorably arrive; the way we prepare for each is important.

154

I have reached the 'Autumn' of my life, both private and public. In the East, there is a theory that we are all born destined to breathe a specific number of breaths before we die; once we have breathed our own ration, off we go! One of the purposes of Yoga is to prolong life by ridding oneself of the passions; the resulting calm will thus spin out the allotted time-span because the breathing will be slower. The performer not only uses his ration in normal living, but also in acting out the passions on stage, passions which to the body, unable to tell the difference between normal and performing emotions, seem absolutely real! The performer therefore draws on his 'breaths' at a faster rate, and my decision to quit opera could be, in the truest sense of the word, a logical act of self-preservation!

I have often heard retired people bemoan the fact that life has in some way 'passed them by'. Some say that life has seemed pointless; they feel they have wasted it. In other words, they have not done what they wanted to do. It is a great tragedy that so many of us, either because of circumstances, family pressure, or the absence of a clear inner direction, find ourselves shunted off into side alleys, into jobs which don't involve us totally as human beings. I don't know what the answer to this problem is. Perhaps the answer doesn't exist, but it does seem so unfair, because fulfilment in work, *any* kind of work, is vital to happiness.

My working years may be shorter than those of most people, but the fulfilment I have always felt will, I truly believe, remain with me in retirement, giving me a sort of 'permission' to enjoy the last part of my life to its utmost. Middle and old age are special times. They are Nature's way of preparing us for the last stage of our development. If things have gone as they should during the other stages in life, the final section is all set for the most important phase of all – the spritual one. It seems to me that the body does its best to release us for this phase by its own ageing.

155

Thursday
22 April   All the cast is in good health, and we are recording again tonight. Masses of gorgeous flowers in my dressing-room, and a pot of *pâté de foie gras* fresh from Strasbourg, brought by some friends from France. The week's break has done us all good and the opera sounds fresh and interesting. I find Mary doing slightly different things, small gestures which grow out of the moment and don't seem to come from *me* at all. Fascinating.

At the end of the evening John Fraser, who is in charge of the recording, tells us with a beaming face that the performance has been so good from everyone they will use tonight as a basic master-tape and correct it from the others.

At 'curtain down' members of the Donizetti Society came onto the stage to present me with the Donizetti Medal, handsomely framed in glass so that both sides can be seen. It will sit on the mantelpiece in my music room. Sir John Tooley and the Christies, up from Glyndebourne, came to greet me most warmly after the short ceremony. We took the Harewoods, who are marvellous company, out to supper. Home, aching with laughter, by 2 a.m.

Friday
23 April   My oldest friend arrives from York. Anne Ellison and I have known each other since we were eleven, and measured our pigtails to see who had the longer hair. She kept hers when the time came to cut them off, and as a treat I persuade her to let me look at the long, shining braids. The hair feels silky, and it is touching to see childhood contained in a small cardboard box. Anne, who was a gentle, quiet little girl with exquisite manners and a kind disposition, is exactly the same now. She is the only friend who goes right back to those early years, my one link with the past; our common memories are precious to me. She takes a great interest in my work and is a real part of our family life. She naturally joins us this weekend to see my final London stage performance.

156

Joan, my beloved sister-in-law, telephones to say plans have altered. Geoff, her husband, is not well, and has been told by the doctor to stay put. She will arrive tomorrow alone, instead of this evening. I am distressed by her news; the occasion without him will be incomplete. We have all shared so many important moments as a family and something will be missing for me. My brother-in-law has a most special place in my affections, and because of a particular act of kindness which he made towards me, an act which took the most tremendous courage on his part to perform, there is a link between us of great significance and on my part, of indescribable gratitude.

The house looks so beautiful in readiness for the guests, with gorgeous flowers everywhere. My loved ones are gathering to support me; I shall need their strength and that of my friends tomorrow night.

Saturday
24 April
There is an article about me in the *Daily Telegraph* by Michael Kennedy, covering my operatic life. It's like reading one's own obituary! Michael, who has been a friend since the Barbirolli days, says he detected in a recent radio interview a note of regret about my decision to quit opera. I am feeling many different emotions this year, but regret is not one of them. Maybe he simply doesn't *want* to believe that any performer in his or her right mind could possibly take this step without regret! I shall certainly miss my theatre life and my theatre friends but that is a different thing altogether. Regret implies a wish to re-consider the decision. I don't.

Into the theatre by 6.45 p.m.; the queue for tickets began at 4 a.m. this morning I am told, they have been changing hands for £100! People come in at intervals to ask how I am, and after feeling emotional all day I am able to reply 'Fine', which is true; as soon as I walked into my dressing room calm descended completely and my mind was filled with nothing but the thought of the job in hand.

Flowers begin to arrive; we fill buckets with water and still they come. Plants all over the dressing-table, presents and greetings from the staff, rose bushes from the chorus, the scent is overpowering. Charles pokes his dear head around the door. He was in Vienna this morning, recording, but got back in the early afternoon. Then John Copley, to greet me for the last time. We are both cheerful and the conversation is light, but he knows and I know that something valuable and important is over; I may well see Charles on the concert platform, I will never work with John again. We can't speak about it, neither do we need to do so. In the theatre people exchange bits of themselves in the work; bits of me are now his and something of him is mine; we walk away, but enriched for always through the many exchanges we have made over a long period of time.

Messages keep coming over the tannoy advising the Company about packing make-up cases and personal effects inside the vans for the journey to Manchester, where they next perform. Not only is this my final night, but the close of the official season as well. I like this feeling of the Company moving North without a break to do other things. It is the end of a phase for me but the opera goes on regardless, as is right and proper; the individual is unimportant.

Act I commences; I can tell the atmosphere out there is electric. People are standing rows deep at the back, they have all come brimming over with good will and a sense of occasion. As the night wears on it is obvious to everyone that this is exactly what our performance is: a great historic occasion in the theatre. The entire cast is rising to the expectation of the audience and every one of the singers is inspired. Instead of finding myself choked with sadness and overwhelmed by emotion, I am savouring every phrase, exhilarated by the sound I am able to produce, transfigured with a joy that makes me feel I could sing another hundred years like this. The house is full of a golden exaltation and we are all sharing in it. What a way to finish my last opera on the London stage. The thrill of such a standard of singing from everyone on such a night is something to cherish for always.

I am literally snowed under with daffodils at my first curtain call, and minutes go by with the thunderous noise of applause. It seems unreal. Lord Harewood comes on to make a delightful, charming, and utterly appropriate speech. This is the hard moment; I hold on to Charles. He knows what I am feeling, and I know that passing through his mind are the many, many moments of marvellous triumphs we have shared together on this stage. How much I owe these two men; what their vision and faith in me have given to me in terms of my development as a performer and achievement as an artist. I had asked for one of the props I use in *Mary Stuart* as a 'goodbye' present, the crucifix which is placed in my hands in Act III. Silvered and pristine, it is presented in a box lined with blue velvet, priceless to me because of the association it bears.

We finally leave the stage and my family join me in the dressing room: Andrew and Sue, my nephew and his wife who have never missed an important occasion, neither of them able to put into words what they are feeling (but I only have to look at their faces to see), Jean, Sue's mother, a loyal and devoted fan, our house-party, Julia, all deeply moved and glad to be sharing this moment with me. It takes a long time to pack away my things, work through an enormous crowd of autograph hunters, and then on to the party given by Lord and Lady Harewood, which finishes off the evening so perfectly. Home to find everyone still up and talking about the events of the night; to bed, finally, at 4 a.m.

Hovering over this great day has been the huge, sombre, powerful presence of Apollo which affected me so deeply as I stood on the stage at Covent Garden. I don't know why he keeps coming into my mind, but he does, and as this second phase reaches its conclusion he is here again, representing something, I believe the profession itself. At one point in the opera Mary Stuart asks Leicester, 'Shall I then regain my freedom?' and I can hear Apollo's voice saying to me, 'Yes, you shall.'

Last night curtain, *Mary Stuart*, with Charles Mackerras

Part Four

Orfeo, Glyndebourne

ORFEO ED EURIDICE

Opera in three acts
Italian libretto by Raniero de' Calzabigi
Music by Christoph Willibald Ritter von Gluck
Producer Peter Hall
Design and Lighting John Bury
Movement Stuart Hopps
Associate Producer Guus Mostart
First night of a new production at Glyndebourne,
27 June 1982

Orfeo Janet Baker
Amor Elizabeth Gale
Euridice Elisabeth Speiser

Harpsichord Continuo
Jean Mallandaine
Glyndebourne Chorus
Chorus Director: Jane Glover
Members of the London Philharmonic Orchestra
Conductor: Raymond Leppard

I imagined there would be a lull in the proceedings like that calm still centre, the 'eye' of a hurricane! Not on your life!

Arriving by post, the costume designs for *Orfeo* land in my lap. After studying the drawings in detail and fingering the samples of material, I reach the conclusion that they are going to look very good. There are minor compromises I want to make, to which I hope Peter (Hall) and John (Bury) will agree.

I have started to read every book on my shelves about the Orphic myths. And here's a strange thing. Who should appear on the scene but my friend Apollo! As god of music, Orpheus was his 'priest'. I knew this but had forgotten. It is not my custom to do much background reading about the characters I play. I prefer to get my information from the score in order to remain true to the composer's ideas, which can be very different from the generally accepted one; Walton's Cressida, for example, is musically speaking, quite far removed from Shakespeare's. The music abounds with a purity and innocence which we don't associate with her. In order to play her as Walton wrote her, I can't allow myself to be brainwashed in any other direction but his. The same with Mary Stuart and Donizetti. But Orpheus is different. In order to understand the many levels of his character I must know something of the ideas he represents, ideas of which Gluck himself must have been deeply aware. Like all the great myths, the simple story has more than one meaning. It will be fascinating to discuss them with Peter and Ray (Leppard).

I recorded a Desert Island Discs programme yesterday, preparing my list of eight records with the greatest difficulty over the weekend; it took many hours because I got side-tracked just sitting listening. Every so often a figure would appear beside me;

it was Keith, having left his desk, unable to keep away from the music!

The choice, dictated by the circumstances of Desert Island restrictions, boiled down to the composers I would be unable to live without (but not all of them – because there are more than eight) plus certain instruments, the harpsichord, the organ and the symphony orchestra. It must be the secret wish of a lot of people to take part in the programme. This is my second, and I was interested to see the list I had chosen on the first occasion; the current one is completely different.

Roy Plumley (another speaking voice of extraordinary richness and beauty) met us in the foyer of Broadcasting House. This famous building is another of those places which are familiar ground to me. I could not begin to count the times I have been there to work in the Concert Hall, deep in the basement.

The first job, across the road in the Library, where there are over a million records, was to play my selection and time them; one is allowed an average of about two minutes per disc. Roy was regaling us with anecdotes about some of his guests, not having record collections of their own, who sit in the studio humming snatches of a half-remembered tune in the hope that one of the team might recognise it; sometimes they don't, and various people from the offices on the same floor are then brought in to see if they can spot the piece of music. Eventually somebody does! Roy leaves a bit of time for this process just in case; my hours of delving at home cut short the time we needed so we sat and drank tea and talked. I signed autographs for the staff and saw old friends from years ago who had been involved with early broadcasts. It was nostalgic and great fun.

The time passed quickly until we had to go back across the road to Broadcasting House and into the tiny studio to record the actual interview. The studios used for music are bigger than those for talking, and this one felt claustrophobic.

Friday We went to hear the students from the National Opera Studio,
30 April who were doing complete scenes from the operatic repertoire
they have been studying this year.

Joined by the musicians of the National Centre for Orchestral
Studies in the pit, with costumes and sets made by the
Wimbledon School of Art, the students treated us to an evening
of musical and visual delight. It is deeply touching and
heartwarming to see young people at work. They gave us many
beautiful moments which proved that when things come off,
youth and inexperience can produce everything necessary to
satisfy an audience. One feels so *glad* for them in their
achievements because the students are at their most vulnerable,
struggling to free themselves from technical limitations. The
evening was particularly helpful to me because I'm going to talk
to them later this month, and it was good to see them first under
fire, so to speak.

Monday Margaret, my husband's mother, arrived this morning. She is a
3 May five foot three, eighty-three year old dynamo. Extensive surgery,
widowhood, and family bereavements have not dimmed her
bright outlook on life; whatever the misfortune, Margaret comes
up smiling. And she is a terrific mother-in-law. It isn't an easy
thing to watch a son marry into 'show business'; she has
accepted the peculiarities of our life, the odd hours, the fact that
my husband actually works for me, and has been totally
supportive of me. I am grateful for this understanding. The
result after twenty-five years is a relationship, not altogether
usual between mothers and daughters-in-law, of real affection.

One of the reasons my marriage has been a happy one is the
common attitude towards life which Keith and I share, the result
of a similar upbringing. Both lots of parents gave us old-
fashioned, but undoubtedly sterling principles; we share a sense

166

of humour, the sort common to Northerners (ripe!), a respect for family life, for money (what you can't afford you can't have!), and ideas which have given us the sense of stability we have needed to balance the insecurities of free-lance work and a life of constant change.

Margaret often says to me with amazement, 'In your position, you might well have moved out of our lives altogether. You needn't ask me here or be nice to me or even speak to me at all!' She genuinely thinks such a course would not only be possible, but quite understandable. It would be possible for us had we not been brought up by parents like ours; but they have to a great extent made us what we are, and all the marvellous things which have happened to us do not make us want to forget our beginnings or deny them.

Margaret loves old films and so do I. We like nothing better than to settle down in front of the television set together, with a rug over our knees, to enjoy a sentimental journey into the 1940's! Margaret's husband Jim died some years ago. He was the sweetest man; extremely good-looking with a wonderful nature. He loved to make people laugh, and would jot down, in a little note-book, any good joke he heard. We all got to know his collection very well indeed and used to encourage him to get his book out every so often by saying, 'Come on Jim, let's have number 63!'

Thursday *6 May* I have recognised the unfamiliar feeling in the pit of my stomach; the last time I remember it was when I walked to school in York with my brother Peter; a bomb had dropped smack in the middle of the building during an air raid the night before. We stood and gazed at the shattered school; the stench, the sight of rubble, the pall over the city, made me realise, even at nine years old, that this was the thing called 'war'. The Falkland

167

Islands may be thousands of miles away, but we are nevertheless affected, not by the physical, but certainly by the psychological aspects of war.

Friday
7 May
To the B.B.C. Television Studios at White City, just twenty minutes away from us by car. My brief appearance on 'Omnibus' takes three hours to get in the can. My make-up girl does what I ask and puts a minimum on my face, which results in what I believe to be a totally natural look. The cardinal rule as one gets older – to use less more efficiently – applies to every day, theatre, or television make-up. The heat of the studio dries up my throat immediately; the wind players in the orchestra have the same trouble. When you see television personalities drinking from a glass of water it is because the air lacks moisture, the vocal chords react speedily and unfavourably to this situation. The hours just standing around under hot lights are tedious, and there is a tension in the air which I think is peculiar to television. The medium produces surface nerves in everyone; the clock is an important factor, so timing is paramount. The staff develop split attention, one ear on the director up in the control box, who communicates to the floor people through an ear phone; the other is left to cope with whatever is actually happening in the studio itself. Whenever one talks to the floor manager or the camera men, one notices this strange glazed look about the eyes which comes from the effort of trying to be in two places at once!

Monday
10 May
A perfect day, riding in the car with Keith and Margaret towards Glyndebourne through English villages bathed in bright sunshine. Oh! this country is wonderful; instead of two months spent working on a new production in a foreign country living in

168

a hotel, I am to enjoy Sussex during the best part of the year.

As we sat in a country lane, sniffing the cow-parsley, and eating a picnic lunch, I thought how much the countryside permeates, in a very real way, every note of music produced at Glyndebourne. Covent Garden is the ultimate in sophisticated elegance, a truly international House. The Coliseum, quite different, a more cosy, homely place, although it seats more people than its elder sister. I feel a great admiration and respect for the former, love for the latter. Both places generate a different atmosphere for performing. Now the Glyndebourne audience has to make a journey through beautiful countryside, by train, car or helicopter! The people come dressed with care, saturated by Nature, fully prepared to compromise between the elegance of the occasion and the informality of a picnic dinner – all things which English people take to like ducks to water. The incongruity of the mixture, the weather risk, everything combines to make an evening of typical English madness. The singers spend weeks soaking up the scenery, breathing in the pollen-laden air, shivering with the cold of our summer, or raving about the beauties of a perfect day. All this goes into the music, it is Sussex and Summer and England. It is the limitless patience and kindness of the Christies and the Glyndebourne staff, some of whom have devoted their entire working lives to the place.

I walked into the courtyard after we had finished our lunch and was immediately swept up into the affectionate cameraderie already established, even this early in the season, by both musicians and administration. I felt as though I had never been away, just as with certain friends, even after a long absence, one feels no separation has taken place.

Janet (Moores) who went to so much trouble to help us find our little flat in Brighton last September, came towards me straight out of the sunlight, smiling, to tell me about final arrangements for our move there at the end of this month. She

169

At Glyndebourne

By the lake at Glyndebourne, with my father and Keith

epitomises the sort of person Glyndebourne attracts; unswerving dedication to everything the work stands for, super-human calm, kindness, and understanding, when the performers begin to grow daily more difficult and strung-up as a first night approaches. I have noticed before how, almost without exception, theatre people on the management side are endowed with the characteristics which help them to hold on firmly when all around is turbulence! They have to cope not only with singers, but artists in every single department of an opera house! Janet has coped and continues to do so, with amazing outward strength. God knows what she and all the other members of the team feel like inside! But they stay, and they support us in innumerable, indispensable ways.

The theatre demands a great deal from everyone involved with it. I suppose we would all say, 'It's worth it'.

A long hard afternoon of concentrated work with the Italian coach Rosetta, and then another journey home, a drive of indescribable beauty. Later, when Margaret kissed me good-night, she said, 'I shall never forget today!' Neither shall I.

Wednesday   The first rose of the year is in bloom; a perfect flower, free from
12 May   disease, a glorious apricot colour. I have put it in a vase beneath the photograph of my mother which is in the music room.

Friday   Margaret returned home this morning. It has been another
14 May   glorious hot day; paradise to sit in the garden, to look at all our freshly cut grass, see the apple trees in the orchard groaning with blossom, and to watch the extraordinary behaviour of an ant colony, moving at tremendous speed, never bumping into each other, crossing and re-crossing a section of the terrace. Viewed from the height of a human being, they look like cars on a motorway, travelling in two directions along a narrow line. I

said, 'I wonder what they'll do when it gets dark?' So Keith replied, 'Switch their lights on, of course!'

We caught the night sleeper to Aberdeen from King's Cross just after 10 p.m. The film team met us on the platform; they want to catch me drinking early morning tea tomorrow! We discussed strategy and parted for the night.

Saturday
15 May
In spite of the smooth ride, I was wakened at 5.30 by two loud-mouthed foreigners, waxing ecstatic over Perth in the early hours of the morning right outside my door. At 6 a.m. the fire alarm went off; it is faulty and no-one has got around to reporting it in strong enough terms for repair. The noise was excruciating, a long drawn-out supersonic whistle which made me clap my hands to my ears in agony. I had ear-ache for hours afterwards. No more sleep of course, so 7.30 found me made-up, and waiting for the camera crew.

I looked at myself in the mirror in my compartment; at such an hour to be up, dressed, and ready to film. Amazing!

Keith was asked to be in on the action; so was the attendant who was, I think, wildly excited to have his activities immortalised. He went coy and had to do his bit over again. What a funny life; drinking early morning tea, looking nonchalantly out of the window, as though I did this every day.

Aberdeen, and a fine morning; we got onto the minibus, together with colleagues from the orchestra who had also journeyed from London on the same train. The drive to Haddo House on such a day was uplifting, and I have never seen it look more beautiful as we swept up to the front door, to be filmed, yet again, being met by June, Marchioness of Aberdeen, and taken into breakfast. I have sung here many times; this great house, now given to the National Trust, was the private home of David and June Gordon and their children when I first came here in the

173

60's. June is a conductor and has by her energy, enthusiasm, and determination, brought music to this area of Scotland, nurturing an interest in it, and providing people with opportunities they would otherwise never have known.

It is a humbling thought to consider just how much is done for the cause of music by a few hard-working, unselfish people. June has struggled with the enormous problems such a venture inevitably brings, backed by the loving, totally understanding support of her wonderful husband David; in so doing she has made of the Haddo concerts not only a valuable cultural contribution to the area, but has given the musicians who take part in them heart-warming memories. Many famous artists have been associated with Haddo. I am sure they believe as I do that it is important to make concerts such as these as much a part of our performing lives as the ones we give in the great international centres throughout the world.

There is an immense joy and privilege in this combination of amateur and professional forces, and June treats her responsibilities with the utmost seriousness and dedication, preparing her work with admirable thoroughness. While such people remain, music is in safe hands.

The weekend is great fun. To those of us staying at Haddo itself, it is like a big house party.

We sleep in the state rooms in four-poster beds, meeting for meals, going for walks on the estate, attending church, bird-watching; to taste a way of life so completely different from the normal run of hotels is a delight.

The kindly, gentle presence of David is now gone from us; the house is full of him still, and on occasions like this especially so, because we who are guests in his home are thinking about him and his immense contribution in support of June.

We had our first rehearsal during the afternoon; our tenor, Neil Jenkins, is stuck somewhere en route, I can imagine him biting his nails and worrying about the outcome of his journey.

174

We rehearsed the Brahms *Alto Rhapsody* and a good deal of Elgar's *Dream of Gerontius*, then broke for tea – the nicest meal in the world; I wish all food could consist of slap-up breakfasts and high teas. This is a Northern tradition, starting with something hot, finishing with something sweet. We had an egg and cheese concoction with sausages and baked beans. Then scones and jam and chocolate cake to finish, all washed down with tea. Scrumptious. It disappeared in no time; there are two groups of people who can make food vanish faster than any other; musicians and ballet dancers. The reason for this is a deep-rooted fear lurking at the backs of our minds that we may never get the chance to eat again; so we make the most of it when it's there! Neil arrived, and gave us the events of his traumatic day, waiting around airports.

I had a break until I was needed again, so Keith and I made for the open and took a walk through glorious country. At a little before 7.45 p.m. which was the time I was due to work again, someone came over to fetch me into the hall. I thought, June must be really cracking on with the rehearsal, she's actually early for Part II. We entered the hall and I made my way to my seat. June put down her baton and started to make a short speech. I looked up in astonishment, because she was thanking *me* on behalf of the Choral Society! I was then presented with a very beautiful water-colour of the house. The little ceremony had been a well-kept secret, and now I have this permanent reminder of all the happy weekends spent here.

Finally, hot soup and then to bed.

Sunday *16 May* We are sleeping in 'Princesses' room. We have been in 'Queens' room and 'State' room before, but this is our favourite because it has the equivalent of the modern twin bed. These are gorgeous mahogany half-testers with blue-and-white curtained canopies and side drapes, lined with plain blue glazed chintz. The bathrooms are next door, so one doesn't have to walk miles away to wash; one isn't aware of traffic along the corridor outside the room because places like Haddo were sensibly built. Of course there is a never-ending battle against cold. High rooms are impossible to heat, and there are certain tricks to be learned in order to cope. Speed is the secret for survival. You get up smartly, run quickly to the bathroom, clean your teeth as the bath water runs, take your clothes off, bathe, put your clothes on again, all in top gear. My theatre training comes in very handy here; people tell me I can change quicker than anyone else in the business, so Haddo is no challenge to me!

One can't be bamboozled by the weather outside either. I always dress as if for winter and then if by chance I feel hot, I can whip off my layers gradually. As a born and bred Northerner you would think my metabolism immune against cold for evermore. But I emigrated to London when I was twenty and have sadly gone soft over the years.

Haddo in May is quite different from Haddo in November. I once did a recital here on a winter Sunday afternoon dressed in June's mink jacket, and in candlelight because there was a power cut.

Even though it is a milder time of the year, there is an electric fire in our bedroom and electric blankets on the beds, so I am as cosy and comfortable as it is possible to be.

The people in the house party here are familiar, kind faces, and everybody spoils me to death. They all come to help either in practical ways or in the choir and orchestra, and have the attitude that those who come to perform must be cherished and cared for, not because of individual importance, but because the music is paramount and everything must be done towards a good result this afternoon. I am on the receiving end of all this care just because I was born with vocal chords of a specific type. I don't deserve it, but by gum I'm making the most of it while it lasts!

176

At 11 a.m. Keith and I went downstairs to meet the film crew, and spent over an hour walking about the estate, shivering in the sneaky wind and trying to be natural.

When lunch time arrived we had a quiet meal with the other two soloists and June, then went our separate ways until the concert at 2.45. The first cars began to arrive, and behold! out came the sun to greet them and the day suddenly turned warm.

It was an afternoon of very special music making, memorable in a singular way; one cannot expect of amateur forces what one hears under other circumstances but there is something heart-warming and deeply touching about performers who do it 'just for love'.

After the concert was over we went into the Library to mingle with people who had made the journey to hear us and were being revived before setting off back home again.

One gentleman bounded up to me beaming:'I've come all the way from Tewkesbury to hear you sing those top A's,' he said, 'and it was worth every mile!'

Eventually everyone left and I did yet more filming in the beautiful morning room, my favourite because it has a marvellous 'family feel' about it.

Then supper, goodbyes, and a car journey to Aberdeen, where the sleeping cars were waiting to take us back to London. Such a happy weekend.

Monday
17 May Emmie Tillett died yesterday, during the afternoon, as far as I can tell, when I was singing the Angel's Farewell at Haddo.

A piece of my life gone for good; that marvellous woman, that indomitable spirit.

She had finished tidying her garden: it was instantaneous. A wonderful way to go.

She was to dine with us on Sunday.

The third person to disappear from my life since this journal

177

began: Edward Boyle; then dear Charles Tapp, founder of the Harrogate Festival, and a great friend both to music and to us; now Emmie. We had made a pact to retire together; but she beat me to it. She was my agent, and she was my friend.

Tuesday We drove to lunch with Gerald and Enid Moore. I have not been
18 May able to see as much of them in the past months as I usually do, particularly since Gerald no longer drives at night; they have been such frequent visitors to us and we have all had many an evening of shop talk and laughter. Gerald and Enid are such good company that we forget how much older than us they actually are.

At home in their beautiful gem of a cottage, in idyllic surroundings, they were at their best today, confident within the confines of their own territory. With a long life of travel behind them, I believe they appreciate the security of home more than ever in these years of retirement; they don't need the outside world any more, having all anyone could possibly want; to look out at superb countryside from their terrace, to see a few dear ones and make superb meals to eat, and when the friends have departed, to settle down by their snug fireside to enjoy each other's company. Enid and Gerald have that rare blessing, a supremely happy marriage, and it is a joy to see.

We had so much to talk about, the hours flew by. The conversation is always the most satisfying mixture of serious music, jokes, and the re-living of shared memories.

We waved 'goodbye' to them, full of delicious food and laughter, in spite of yesterday's sad news.

Wednesday A busy day, but in the evening a visit to my nephew Andrew and
19 May his wife Sue; he is Keith's sister's son and a doctor, married to another doctor. They live only half-an-hour's drive away from

us, and are about to celebrate their second wedding anniversary. In spite of tremendously busy work schedules, and studying for further qualifications, they have put their house and garden in immaculate order and proudly entertain their friends and family.

It is a very pleasant thing to be an aunt, driving to supper with one's nephew and niece; I can't quite take in the fact that Andrew is all grown up though! This peculiar thing called 'time' seems to play strange tricks with people one has watched from babyhood.

A few weeks ago Andy went to get some petrol from a garage and came back with a barbecue! (I think he got petrol as well.) He decided to invite us to dinner out of doors. We looked at all the plants in the garden, (very interesting) had our drinks, also a delectable first course, and then our host got cracking with the steaks. After some time, we got the distinct impression that he wished he had just stuck to buying petrol at his garage, and at one point he disappeared completely in smoke! But eventually all was ready, and we unanimously agreed that steaks took on an extra dimension cooked out of doors on charcoal. A first-rate dessert and coffee to follow. It was a night to put aside thoughts of calories and just enjoy food!

Later, talking of their work, it was deeply touching to hear them speak with such compassion, both for the sick people they are trying to heal and also for their families. Andrew is veering towards the treatment of cancer which he describes as a most exciting field; Sue is a G.P. They both remarked on the importance of the family attitude where this terrible disease is concerned.

Here are two people, just married, having set up their first home, worked hard at it, begun to grow things in their garden, engrossed in work of the most demanding and fulfilling kind, and caring deeply for the people they meet in the course of it; in other words, two people steeped in the 'old fashioned' ideas of

179

marriage, home, and service to others: they are not alone in their ideals, many of their friends are similarly absorbed. We read so much about youth unemployment, drug abuse, vandalism, and the terrible cruelties arising from frustration and boredom; it is so good to see the other side of the coin. Their lives are just beginning, the middle-aged are taking stock, and the old die: it has a beautiful sense of order, rightness, and pattern. The circle which is not quite a circle but a spiral, and each end contains another beginning.

Friday A warm day, but over-clouded. We left the house early to arrive
21 May in good time at Marylebone Cemetery, allowing for heavy rush hour traffic. Emmie's cremation service was due to begin at 10 a.m. But first I went out into the garden to pick the most beautiful rose I could find. Although we had arranged for a professional wreath of white flowers, I felt so strongly that there should also be a real garden flower; she loved gardens and flowers so much. I found a bloom which was ideal, wrapped it up in a damp cloth, and put it into the car. There were so many famous and familiar faces. The service has nothing to do with the departed, it seems to me, but everything to do with the people who attend. We greeted everyone and went into the little chapel. I had asked the attendant if it would be possible for my rose to be put on the coffin but Emmie's brother, as chief mourner, was the only person who could give permission and I decided I could not possibly bother him with my request. The attendant took me up to the far end of the building and, pointing to a marble shelf, said, 'Why don't you put your flower on the floor just here.' I did so, and was perfectly content to know that it would at least be near Emmie during the service. It was all quite short, simple hymns and prayers and some words spoken by Joseph Cooper. We sat there with our private memories and feelings, each in his own way saying a personal and individual 'goodbye' to our old friend.

180

No matter how firm our faith, the painful, raw facts of death are impossible to bear.

After the service we filed out to look at the lovely flowers everyone had brought. They made a glorious sight spread out in the sunlight; we said our farewells and continued our subdued journey into London, where we had a rather special luncheon date. This had been arranged by my publisher and great friend Julia MacRae, who had offered to cancel when she heard the news about Emmie. I would not consider that, firstly because the event had been planned well ahead and cancellation would have greatly inconvenienced the other guests, secondly because Emmie herself would have disapproved; I could imagine her saying, 'Now, my dear, just carry on with your life quite normally. This is nothing to make a fuss about!'

Julia had chosen her guests carefully; her object was to introduce me to friends who had been extremely supportive of her new venture into a wider area of publishing and to two people who had read the first part of my manuscript some months previously, Christine Pevitt of Book Club Associates, who had immediately bought the book club rights, and Peter Crookston from the *Observer,* who had bought serial rights for the *Observer* Magazine. Christine Pevitt's initial reaction, after seeing only a few pages, had been of the greatest encouragement to me in those early days, and I was particularly glad to have the opportunity to tell her so and to thank her. John Hyams of W.H. Smith, John Welch and John Cheshire from Heffers (who had come specially from Cambridge), Simon Bainbridge from Hatchards, and Zoë, completed our party.

Julia had found a most delightful spot for lunch, a small, extremely elegant private suite at The English Garden restaurant just off the King's Road. We walked up the stairs into a charming sitting-room and greeted our hostess. Within ten minutes everyone had arrived.

We stood for a little while chatting comfortably and someone brought up the subject of book titles and asked why I had chosen *Full Circle* for mine? I began to explain the circumstances which had prompted me to write, and said that the book should really be called *Full Spiral*, because although the year I'm living in right now is indeed a series of endings, or closed circles completing themselves, it is also turning out to be a series of new beginnings; the very fact of my standing in a room talking to a group of people who were not musicians but members of a different profession, and feeling myself totally at ease with them, was a case in point. I am very experienced in this sort of situation – meeting strangers, exchanging conversation, and parting again. They are usually events from which one walks away totally drained of energy, and time so spent seems wasted. As we went into the adjoining dining-room and began our meal, it was obvious to me that this occasion was different; not only was I having an extraordinarily good time, but in some subtle way I felt 'accepted' by these people. Even though only two of them had read any of the manuscript, the kind of respect they were all according me was not just that given to a famous singer; I was being treated as a person who had something to do with their world too. I have never felt such a sharing, except with those of my own profession when talking shop. This talk was of books and writing: I was at home in it and at home with them. We ranged between Iris Murdoch, Jane Austen and Arthur Ransome with no trouble at all; John Welch asked me at one point what my next book was going to be, as though it was the most natural thing in the world for him to assume there was going to *be* a next one. When I had recovered from his question and replied that most probably I had only *this* book inside me, he answered, 'You don't seem to me like a one-book person!'

The meal progressed and so did the laughter and the stories. I have always loved books; I was now finding that the people who deal with them as a livelihood were just as fascinating and enjoyable! We were all sitting around the table for no reason other than to enjoy each other's company, linked by the common interests of books and music. We parted mid-afternoon, replete with wonderful food and conversation.

As we drove home, my mind went back to the evening last October, when Julia, having discussed the idea with her staff, decided to pluck up the courage to talk to me about a book which she badly wanted to bring out to mark the finish of my operatic career. She felt deeply that the season of 1982–83 should be recorded in some way, and with great hesitation she began to tell me her idea. This was to gather together photographs of all my operatic roles and to do a picture-book with a linking commentary by a professional writer. She told me later that during this explanation I had a strange expression on my face which she put down to the fact that I was finding the whole subject distasteful! She had known about the requests from other publishers asking me to write an autobiography, with the offer of a ghost writer to help me. She also knew exactly what I thought of these requests! When Julia had finished, I said to her, 'I think I ought to tell you that I have begun to write something myself. I started a journal at the end of September because I felt I wanted to keep a record of my thoughts and feelings during this year. I meant to give you the first bit of manuscript at Christmas in case you were interested in publishing it.' Now it was her turn to look odd! She just could not believe that I had made such a decision and had actually started to write. I repeated my well-worn comments about my lack of interest in the usual autobiographical form and told her that the urge to put down my ideas could only work in journal form, so I had decided to start before *Alceste* and finish after the last night of Glyndebourne. 'Thank God you didn't wait until Christmas to tell me,' she said. 'We've got to get this organised right away, because it must come out next Autumn.'

We discussed at length the complications involved in meeting deadlines; we also talked about the importance of the right photographs, and I told her the person I wanted on the project was Zoë Dominic; we agreed that to have the pictures done by one person would give the book a unity of style. Julia also asked me to re-consider very carefully my decision to give the book to her for publication, pointing out that although she had begun to publish a general list this year, her reputation had been made in the area of children's books, and a larger, older-established firm might be a wiser choice for me. I did not see why I should go to another publisher though; Julia is a very good one, and she is also my friend. All publishing houses have certain books offered to them because of personal loyalties; it is a perfectly acceptable state of affairs.

The autobiography of a public figure may hold the attention of the reader for an hour or so, merely as a curiosity. From the beginning I wanted my journal to be something more than that – not just my own story told in my own words, but an attempt to work towards a greater understanding of my profession in the hearts of those who might read it. I also hoped it would be a piece of good writing. The decision to begin came from the same deep place within me which houses the instincts I have as a musician. That I *have* to sing and sing in a certain way, is dictated to me by this unconscious urge and I obey it. I *must* sing, and now I feel I *must* write.

The total confidence I felt in placing myself in the hands of my friend have been, as the months passed, completely justified. I wonder if ever a book has been put together in such an extraordinary way? From scribbled note-books, filled with my atrocious writing, we go to typed pages, transcribed not only by Julia herself, but also by Delia, Linda and Rosemary, her un-flappable, admirable, wonderful colleagues. Zoë, after bouts of photographic sessions, produces pictures so beautiful it is hard to confine ourselves to the limits determined by the size of the book. Douglas Martin, the designer, whom I have not yet met but who sounds like a soul-mate, takes proofs of the edited typescript and hands over mock-ups of the design which delight the eye. I look in amazement at the words in print and wonder where on earth they are all coming from; the book is indeed being written, and by me, but the feeling of holding in my hands a concrete product of my inner ideas is something new to me, and exhilarating beyond words. Everyone involved shows immense concern and care, including, of course, Julia's production director, Rita Ireland, and the printers in Hampshire. I am allowed a vote, even in decisions such as the final jacket design; to a singer, who has never had any say whatsoever in a single record sleeve, it is all heady stuff; So far all the deadlines are being met on schedule; I am terrified in case I dry up and have to say, 'Sorry, I can't think of any more.'

Keith and I both felt weary after arriving home that evening. It had been an emotional day and we went to bed early. My last thought was of the deeply touching moment when Emmie's coffin was placed on the marble support where it stood for the entire service, red roses from the family resting upon it. As one of the bearers stepped back, he suddenly bent down, picked up my rose from the floor, and placed it beside the wreath on the coffin, directly above her face. She would have liked that.

Wednesday 26 May A glorious summer morning. Florence arrived at nine, it is her day for working here. We all sat out on the terrace for coffee, gazing at the garden in general and the oak tree in particular; it is hundreds of years old and we feel that it is the genuine resident, not us. Standing about fifty yards away from the house, its feet planted firmly in the ground, it is master of all it surveys. 'I bet that tree's seen some sights,' Florence said. My father told us he heard a cuckoo yesterday, and looking at me, said, 'Do you remember — ?' 'Yes,' I replied, 'I *do* remember', knowing exactly to what he referred. A long time ago, when Peter and I were small – he would have been about eleven and I eight – my

185

parents decided to take us for a picnic. We didn't have a car and Peter was in his wheel-chair at the time; because of his heart complaint there were long periods when he couldn't walk. So off we went, my father and mother taking turns to push the chair and my little legs trotting by the side. The spot we were making for was about three miles away and by the time we got there it seemed to me like thirty-three! My mother had gone to a lot of trouble preparing the food; the whole thing was quite an adventure. When we started out, the day was fine; by the time we arrived the sky was looking overcast. We spread out the picnic, and sure enough, down came the rain, not just a shower, it poured and showed no sign of letting-up. We sadly gathered the tea things together and made for the nearest hedge. It was a gully, with overhanging branches, so we sat there, rain pelting down, eating soggy sandwiches and wishing we were home, dry and warm. Suddenly a bird, which had seen us sheltering in the thick foliage, perched about ten feet away and began to sing – 'Cuckoo, cuckoo.' The damn bird was loud and cheeky, quite clearly saying, 'What are you silly fools doing here, eating your tea in a hedge bottom in the pouring rain?' It occurred to us that perhaps we *did* look a rum sight and we all began to laugh. I have never heard the song of a cuckoo without thinking of that moment; neither, it appears, has my father!

I lunched with my friend Margaret Sampson. I shall be away until August once Glyndebourne begins, with only the odd day at home, so it was good to have the opportunity to talk. Human friendship, at its deepest level, is perhaps the most important factor in our lives. It is the one relationship which keeps a space between people; what is given in friendship is always a bonus because no-one owes anybody anything, or wants anything, there are no duties involved; one is quite free.

I came home and went straight out to do some gardening. We are trying to get everything in marvellous order before we depart for Sussex next Monday. I have seen my favourite rose out, also the azaleas and the rhododendrons. I resent leaving the garden for so long, but it is the last time; in future my summers will be arranged differently – there won't be any long periods away. When one is young, career must come first, but I am glad the time has arrived for me when the blooming of a favourite flower is too precious an event to miss.

Saturday 29 May We drove north to dine with my sister- and brother-in-law, trying to fit a family occasion with a recital at Mold. I nearly didn't get there at all! A frantic telephone call came from San Francisco, asking me to sing the opening performance of *Julius Caesar* with the old team from the Coliseum production; something radical had gone wrong with plans at the Opera House and they were desperate. I could not, with the best will in the world, jeopardise the recital, planned two years ago, or disappoint my audience. Besides that, what sort of physical shape would I have been in, tackling such a journey twice in less than a week and then having to turn up, fresh as a daisy, at Glyndebourne on Tuesday morning? The daisy would have been wilting, I suspect. Anyway, the answer was 'No'. The Director of San Francisco said to Keith over the phone, 'It would be rather fun for her to appear here in her final operatic year.' Fun!

Our family dinner included Andrew and Sue, up for the weekend, and friends who came complete with their son, daughter and four month old grand-daughter, who was as good as gold when allowed to join in the merriment, but who took a dim view of the situation when put to bed. Her mother wisely allowed her to sit up and enjoy herself. The son we have known since childhood, and it is a strange feeling to see yet another generation sprouting – but rather nice too. After all, Keith and I *could* be grand-parents! We left shortly after the meal for Chester where we stayed the night in order to be on hand for Mold the following

187

morning; we had arranged to meet the organisers at 11 a.m. in order to come to some compromise over the acoustics.

Sunday Another gloriously hot morning – the countryside looking its
30 May fabulous best. Exactly a year ago, while holidaying in this part of the country with Joan and Geoff, we had made a detour to see the Clwyd Theatre; perched high on a hill overlooking the town of Mold, it is an excellent building extremely popular with audiences, who drive there to have a meal in the restaurant and spend a pleasant evening at the theatre. Although ideal for the spoken word, I immediately felt that there was not enough resonance in the auditorium for a good musical sound, and I later telephoned Michael Grensted who couldn't have been more sympathetic. We decided to meet on the morning of the concert to make some experiments. He was there to greet us, and so were the members of his technical staff. They had rigged up an acoustic screen which we tried in one position. I then asked them if it could be moved back about ten feet. They said, 'Yes, it could well take us fifteen minutes. Go and have a coffee and we'll call you when we've finished.' The coffee already percolating in my flower-filled dressing room was soon ready and we took our cups outside to drink it and look at the view. The screen in its new position was a definite improvement, so we decided to settle for that. Later that evening when I returned for the recital, the stage had been discreetly lit, and large flower arrangements placed at each side; the whole thing looked really good. The sound was still far from ideal, but possible; the help and understanding we had received from everyone involved was heart-warming. The organisers could not have done more to try and meet my wishes, and afterwards they gave us a buffet supper so that I could have a few relaxed moments with the family, who had come to the concert, before we set off for London. The Welsh have a great respect for the voice, being not only good singers themselves but possessing impeccable manners

188

in a Green Room. They actually appear to enjoy what you have been doing and come in, look you straight between the eyes, shake you warmly by the hand, say 'Thank you' as though they mean it, and depart without more ado, giving the artist a fair opportunity to talk to each person. I mention this 'perfect' Green Room behaviour because it is unusual and is deeply appreciated by the performers. The events which happen to me back stage would not only fill another book, but would never be believed by my readers!

Full to the brim with pork pie and sausage rolls, we said our farewells and started the long drive home. I'm *glad* I didn't go to San Francisco!

Monday   It *is* hard to leave my garden on a day like this. We spent most of the
31 May   morning getting all the things we need for the next eight weeks, favourite pans, the typewriter, Keith's papers, together with clothes and music.

Then we enjoyed what was left of the time sitting outside, looking at the view and finally saying our 'goodbyes' to the rhododendrons and azaleas. I know it's here waiting for me to come back to, but that thought doesn't really help. A hug for my father and then we're away, Keith nursing the car very carefully with all the extra weight.

Wherever I go in England I am continually saying to myself, 'This really is the most beautiful country in the world.' In spite of an enormous amount of travel, I have still managed to do most of my working right here, an unusual and fortunate state of affairs for a singer.

We arrived at the little flat we had chosen so long ago last September and found it scrupulously clean, tidy, ready for occupation, and prettier than I remembered. We unpacked, went for a short exploration, finding all the shops we needed within two minutes, and then tumbled into bed.

189

A day of music with Raymond Leppard and Martin Isepp, who is wearing yet another hat, as Head of Music Staff. Ray has anticipated all my problems. We were in the Green Room, a long, wood-panelled gallery so familiar to me. As usual when absorbed, the hours passed quickly. During coffee breaks and lunch I met many old friends, familiar faces. Elizabeth Harwood, my beloved colleague in a number of vintage Scottish Opera productions, is here to play the Marschallin in *Rosenkavalier*. I have known her practically all my working life, and since she is from Yorkshire we have a similar sense of humour and outlook on life. She is devoted to her family and is not only a beautiful woman but has the priceless gift of charm. On many occasions, I have seen Elizabeth completely change a tricky situation; to be an absolute knock-out physically is, of course, a great help, but she has besides a genuinely kind and loving personality allied to immense tact and a pleasant way of persuading people to do things! She can charm the birds off the trees and there is no-one in the world I would rather work with. How lovely to have her, if not in my opera at least in the vicinity.

Ray is a Leo as I am; his character has many aspects which are familiar to me because I recognise myself in them. I cannot count the occasions when we have worked together, in the opera, in concert, or in the recording studio; I cannot count the endless ways in which he has influenced my musical life, or the occasions when our collaboration has produced that special kind of magic which makes not only music but the whole of life worth while.

It is fitting that he should be directing my last opera performances from the pit.

When we met for lunch Keith informed me that people are beginning to look older! He gazed at me in astonishment when I pointed out that perhaps they thought the same about us!

It all seems a far cry from my early chorus days when Anthony Besch produced me in *Magic Flute* (and in many subsequent productions over the years); he told me recently that he had seen

190

With Raymond Leppard

the remark *Baker : palm* written in a notebook. In those days it was a treat to be given something to hold, or something to do, even in this most minor way, to enliven the duties of a humble chorus member. Anthony was my very first producer; for the many years of our collaboration he continued to help, teach and discipline, always demanding a great deal but giving back just as much to his singers. He was the person responsible for casting me as Dorabella in Scottish Opera's famous production of *Cosi fan Tutte* with Elizabeth as Fiordiligi. To everyone's amazement (except Anthony's) I proved capable of comedy, my image as a serious

191

non-smiling oratorio singer shattered for ever! Both he and Colin Graham, with whom I worked a lot at Aldeburgh, were typical of the British opera scene in the fifties and sixties. They encouraged team work, expected us to act, not just stand about the stage being singing machines. The preparation they did, the quiet kindness of their behaviour, set the tenor of my own expectations of theatre people, and I owe much of my confidence to them and certainly my early development as a 'stage animal'. All the producers I've ever worked with have allowed me freedom to preserve my own space in which to 'be' a character, although obeying implicitly whatever was asked of me as a member of a team. I have never learned 'how' to act. I do not believe it is necessary if one is sufficiently immersed in the character. 'Sufficiently' is, however, the key word; it implies months of private, interior work and total concentration in production. It is a high price to pay, but the end result is the only one worth striving for. Even when I came to work with Götz Friedrich at Covent Garden I found to my surprise that he granted me this privilege, leaving me alone to work out my own salvation, after first searching for, and discussing, the character together. He had a reputation for being a 'difficult' producer, and I thought he would certainly put me in a straitjacket, but he did nothing of the kind, and I felt he respected the sort of performer I was; at the same time, I learned a great deal from him.

Carl Ebert, whom we chorus members thought of as 'god', dominated Glyndebourne in my first year there. He looked like a god too! Incredibly handsome, power sat very well on him. I wish *so* much that I had eventually reached the stage of working with him as a principal; I think he must have been pleased as the years went by, to see the change in opera singers as they gradually rose to the challenge of ever higher expectations. Gone, I hope for ever, are the days when a singer can stand on stage and rely only on a beautiful sound: today, a completely rounded performance, visually and histrionically, is the norm. Carl Ebert must have been one of the great innovators in this respect; he brought from the straight theatre (he was a marvellous actor) a new standard; even watching him, as I tried to do whenever possible, I felt his passionate concern, his delight when a singer succeeded in the demands made, his displeasure when things did not go right. I later worked with his son Peter, who was responsible for the stunning *Trojans* we did for Scottish Opera and for the production of *Orfeo* in 1978. We talked about Carl Ebert and the effect he had on us all in 1956, and Peter had many wise and wonderful things to say about his father.

Wednesday 2 June The best moments are never for the audience – they are for us! We all meet in the organ room: (where performances were given before the Opera House was built) chorus, production staff, designer, principals, and conductor, to have what Sir Peter Hall calls his 'preparatory talk'. In he comes, a tall, commanding figure, beaming with delight at everybody. I did not have Carl Ebert as a principal but I do have Peter Hall – another man of the 'real' theatre, and oh! what a privilege and delight it is! Peter likes to give us at the onset, before we set foot on the production floor, the main idea behind his conception of the characters – a motif or theme; the words he speaks to us about *Orfeo* are beautiful, inspiring, and immediately bind us together as a team. It is an important moment, significant and deeply moving. Ray speaks about the score and then we are shown the model of the set, which John Bury explains to us. We make our way to the rehearsal stage to begin. It is like the start of an adventure, an exploration, a journey, which we are making together. The first step is the hardest.

The play, acting, and actors are my great joy. I go to the theatre to be totally immersed, without any responsibility, in another world. There is nothing for me to do except sit and be showered with delight, wonder, pain, new ideas. I feel such a debt towards the stage 'proper' and what is achieved there, such a sense of

193

gratitude and reverence towards all those involved. I have learned a great deal about my own job, sitting in a theatre.

To work with Peter, one of the great directors of our time, coming as he does from that other world, has been the peak experience for me as a singer-actress. He has brought so much to us. I asked him recently if he had found his experience a two-way communication? In other words, had he taken back to his actors anything from us? He replied with a definite affirmative, and I saw concrete evidence of this when I went to a performance of the *Oresteia* recently.

It is unfair to abstract from all the wonderful hours I have spent watching plays moments of special significance, because I cannot remember a single occasion when I have left a theatre unmoved, or unchanged. But there are two mind-blowing experiences which I would not have missed; one was the RSC's *Nicholas Nickleby* and the other the National Theatre's *Oresteia*. The *Oresteia* are, as all masterpieces should be, for 'Now'. At many levels they speak to us and they speak straight to the heart. I sat in the Olivier Theatre last week, and as the hours passed the masks worn by the actors seemed to take on expressions of indescribable beauty and pathos, with a strange, almost menacing intensity. They made me feel as though I sat totally alone in the audience, and that they were all looking right at me! The immediacy of the idioms, every word, every gesture, seemed to be meant personally. The actors' amazing achievement in combining complicated speech with equally complicated musical rhythms provided by the orchestral players, was a miracle of timing. I could only imagine the amount of killing work involved.

It was especially helpful to share this experience just before starting in *Orfeo*; these archetypes are people I know well, and who should figure large on the scene but my friend Apollo!

In a miniature way, Orfeo's journey as a man mirrors the journey of Agamemnon's family, back to the light of day, after horrendous trials and tribulations.

194

With Peter Hall

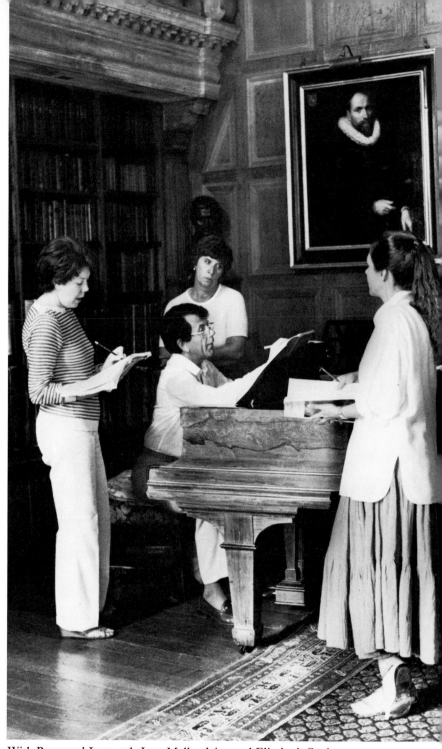

With Raymond Leppard, Jean Mallandaine and Elisabeth Speiser

Thursday
3 June

An interesting morning with the chorus. These young people are the cream; they perform as individuals; as yet they all feel, with justification, that they stand a good chance of 'making it' in this profession. Quite a few of them undoubtedly will. All have the basic equipment – circumstances of health, opportunity, and good luck, will decide the rest. But because they each have hearts full of hope and unspoiled enthusiasm, their power as a group is sensational. It is not only a question of beautiful sound, but an attitude of mind. We worked together this morning, and even at such an early stage, something magical has already begun to happen. It will be shattering in performance.

At the morning break for coffee and at lunch, everywhere one turns there are welcoming, familiar, and affectionate faces. There is nothing quite like the atmosphere created by talented people engrossed in work they love; beautiful surroundings and the sun smiling down upon us are a bonus.

My father arrived at lunch time. I hope the change and the sea air will do him good. At home he never smokes his pipe in our part of the house; here in the flat his bedroom, a pleasant room overlooking the square gardens to the sea, is his territory, so he can smoke himself to death in there!

Keith's papers and typewriter already look quite at home, in fact, we have settled down quickly. The glorious weather helps.

I managed to find time to join the Lewes Library on the way home today. Couldn't bear to be without a proper supply of books!

Friday
4 June

It was 'break through' day today. Ray, Peter, Elisabeth Speiser (my sweet Euridice) and I spent a hard morning in the organ room, going over and over the scene of the journey back to the upper world, an extremely difficult one. There is always more than one way of playing a scene. The experiments continued today until we found the key which suited us best, slowly discovering an interpretation which made the actions work; we

197

found it where the answers are always to be found if one looks hard enough – in the score.

Peter likes to sketch in the entire piece, giving us a water-colour to think about. As the days go by, the water-colour will change until by the first night we shall have a rich oil painting in our hands.

John Bury has conceived a pathway which seems to stretch backwards from the pit to infinity and all the action takes place upon it. Unfortunately the wall of the rehearsal room does not extend as far back as the stage area does, so we are working with a piece of equipment which is roughly fifteen feet shorter than the actual size. This is causing us problems of orientation; it won't be easy to feel at home when we do have the stage, late next week. As *Orfeo* is the third production of the season we have to share stage time with *Rosenkavalier* and the two operas which are already on.

After the day's work is done and supper over, Keith and I have been walking by the sea, just as I imagined we would, but instead of cold winds and an angry sea, Brighton, basking in a heatwave, feels like the Mediterranean; late at night the water is calm as a mill pond; people and dogs swim in it until darkness falls. We have awakened each morning to cloudless skies. It can't last.

Saturday 5 June It's scorching even before breakfast. We haven't had any of the bad storms which brought torrential rain to other parts of the country.

We fled to another rehearsal room to escape the sounds of *Rosenkavalier*; it just doesn't go with Gluck somehow! We stumbled along this morning, taking in new ideas, both musical and dramatic, feeling as though blindfold, hobbled, walking over hot bricks! It is a familiar stage and soon passes. After a canteen lunch (very good food this year), we met the chorus in the big

198

rehearsal room where we have the basic set; it was stifling even with all the windows open.

'We're going to run through the whole opera this afternoon,' Peter announced. 'I know it will be a mess but it will help us all to get a general idea. So don't worry if you can't remember what we did the other day.'

The chorus overwhelm me, they give so much; I look into the young, eager, hopeful faces and see myself twenty-odd years ago. They look at me and see – What? – I don't know. Someone who has had success, fulfilment, who still loves the work – all of these things goals worth striving for. We stand on stage and get to know one another, they are gradually beginning to feel able to touch me freely, they were shy at first and that was beautiful too.

I had a costume fitting today; John's design for me makes me *look* exactly as Peter has suggested I should *feel*. Now that is as good a result as you could hope to achieve! Sunday is a free day so we drove back to London in the evening to spend a night or two at home.

Sunday 6 June The grass in the orchard and vegetable garden is two feet high. We got stuck in as soon as the thunderstorm passed. When we first came to this house we pondered long and hard about the kind of grass-cutter we should buy. The land slopes away downhill from the house, so a sit-upon was out of the question – we should have rolled off! Keith was talking to his cousin Christopher Slack (Phil and Hilda's son) who has similar problems. 'Got to get a Mountfield, old boy,' he said. So we did. We got two actually – identical, so I start mine and Keith starts his and we meet somewhere in the middle. I don't like disturbing the neighbours on Sunday, but we have to make the most of this opportunity. We could employ a gardener but we like to do it ourselves. Very therapeutic swinging away at nettles; besides which, we reckon we can do it better and faster than anybody

199

else! Once we make up our minds to do a particular job out there, we get into our gardening togs and set to like a couple of whirlwinds. My mother-in-law watches us in amazement when she's here. After we've finished we sit on the terrace, gaze out at the tidy scene, and pat ourselves on the back!

It is good to have some breathing space from the opera. As we drove through London on the way home it was like getting back to the normal world. Glyndebourne is a very possessive mistress. Once in her clutches she holds you tightly to her bosom and says, 'You belong to me. Just forget about everything else' – and you do! For concentrated work, it is perfect, and I see now very clearly where my decision not to do opera beyond these shores came from. It came from Glyndebourne in 1956. I started opera in the best possible circumstances, although I didn't know it at the time, and the experience left its mark. Every opera I did subsequently, I must have compared with that first experience. Aldeburgh was different, but in terms of care, time and standard very like, although the facilities couldn't compare.

I understand, absolutely, that the repertoire opera houses cannot work like this, and I accept the fact; but I was determined not to allow myself to be swept up exclusively into this way of working and I have never regretted this decision.

I have had valuable conversations with Peter and Ray about the way I should play this role. I thought of Orfeo as a hero; a son of the gods, a priest of Apollo, and man who represents the power of music and its communication to the people. Peter wants a very much more human and simple approach. He sees the character as a shepherd, making the journey to Hades to find his wife and bring her back to the light of day. He sees him as open, rather naive, and vulnerable. I had been singing the recitative sections 'to myself' – that is, addressing them to myself. I am being encouraged to direct my attention to Euridice, the gods, the chorus, and the audience; I am to tell the audience exactly what I am feeling, making them share with me every step of the

200

way. Orfeo thus goes through the emotions of the situation *for* the audience, and in telling them what is happening to him, involves them. The stage has an apron which takes me close to the audience, so that even physically I shall feel close to them and they to me. It is the medium thing all over again; this time, I am transmitting music, but am also asked to fire the emotions for the audience too. I am literally saying, 'Here I am as Orfeo, trying to find a part of myself (Euridice) who is lost to me. We all know what that means. Every one of us is in some way incomplete. I am making this journey to find wholeness so that I can be a truly 'human' being, a unified one, not a collection of different bits and pieces. As I undergo the journey up here on the stage, I am showing you that you too are on the same journey. You too have to tame the inner fears, make friends with your demons, and be finally really alive when the inner turmoils are conquered.' The reason Orfeo or anyone else starts the journey is Love. It is the only power which can bring us safely through.

Monday
7 June
Orfeo has a physical 'symbol' – his lyre, brought to him from Apollo by Amor. It has seven strings – seven is the sacred number of Apollo and strangely, my age this year is a perfect multiple of seven. I am forty-nine years old in August! I like to have a prop which I must use a lot, right there to hand on the very first day. I wanted my lyre, and there it was waiting for me. I picked it up and promptly dropped it again: it weighed a ton! 'I can't use that,' I said, 'it's far too heavy.' John Bury's face looked wistful but he realised at once that I couldn't carry it around and sing as well. It is full size and made of beautifully marked ash wood. As the days have passed I have continually picked it up, put it down (it rests on its own base on the floor for some of the time), slung it over my shoulder, stroked it, and even cursed it when it has become too heavy. Gradually it is assuming a powerful life of its own. People ask to try its weight and I hand it to them. They are always shocked

201

that I have something so heavy. The props department are busy making me a new one in balsa-wood, but I am not at all sure that I want to discard this one. We shall see.

Tuesday
8 June
The Royal Academy of Music has an association attached to it called the RAM Club. The members have a dinner at the Royal Lancaster Hotel tonight and I was invited, together with Keith, to be the guest of honour and make a speech; since it is the Principal's final term at the RAM. I agreed to do so; Sir Anthony and Lady Lewis have been friends of ours for over twenty years. I don't enjoy making formal speeches; answering 'off the cuff' questions from an interviewer or an audience is different, and I do enjoy that, very much. This evening, many things needed to be said about Tony and Lesley Lewis and I wanted to get it right. It's a responsibility. Our relationship, musical and personal, is of such long standing and he has influenced me greatly, both musically and personally. I could make a long, long list of all the people I have ever worked with; from the great majority I have gained knowledge, a few have provided me with negative experiences. I owe every single one of them a debt of gratitude because they have all taught me *something*. But it was good to have this opportunity to express what many of us feel about a fine musician and a wonderful person.

Thursday
10 June
A long hard morning, on stage for the first time; we spent the entire session putting some sense into the final scene, which entails a bit of complicated movement and the passing from hand to hand of enormous garlands. We weaved back and forth with the poor old gods perched on step ladders, getting in our way. Eventually they will be suspended but at the moment they are, with respect, a damn nuisance! Next, dancing lessons; we've all got to dance!

203

A useful music call; Ray never lets us get too far away from the music – we are like strong-willed horses gradually being broken in, properly reined and bridled. Let's hope we turn out to be thoroughbreds!

Friday
11 June

Elisabeth Speiser and I had to be fitted into the movements of the dance which all the chorus already know. So choreographer, Stuart Hopps, had us both to himself and with the help of two of his dancers, put us through our paces.

Now singing and acting are strenuous affairs, but compared with dancers, singers don't know they're born! We counted and danced and counted and sweated and over and over again. We did it feeling like baby elephants next to the fairy-light creatures who were teaching us the steps – for the first hour it was great fun. But after that I started to wonder just how these frail creatures keep it up hour after hour, day after day. Dancers always practise in odd corners. You bump into a lifted leg in the dark and wonder what on earth it is until you suddenly realise its a limb being limbered up! But the next minute, you see the same frail bodies wolfing down huge sandwiches and glasses of milk at the coffee break, and believe me they deserve every single calorie. I wouldn't be a dancer for all the tea in China; they are overworked, underpaid, and the kindest people ever involved in an opera house.

We picked up the dance pretty quickly, but heaven knows what we look like doing it. My Euridice is a slight person so she made a pretty picture. I shall just hope the flying folds of my Orfeo cloak will hide the movements of my flying feet!

Saturday
12 June

We had the stage again. Everything feels completely different out there compared with the rehearsal room. Today the iron grilles were used; they form the gates of Hades, and when I first

204

see them they are alive with moving figures crawling all over the surface. It's a grim sight. The chorus has a lot of vigorous movement, jumping, running, leaping – they are supposed to be menacing animals and I am supposed to be in fear of them. When the set is lit and we are in battle conditions, there won't be any 'supposed' about it. The scene will be formidable and so will they.

As I gradually soothe them by music, they all take on a gentler aspect, and this situation, which greatly moved me when they first did it, is now developing in a marvellous way.

We find it tiring, three hours of repeating the 'Hades' scene over and over again; the singers get out of breath with running, and we all make thankfully for the canteen and lunch. The film team has arrived; the cameras began to turn this afternoon in the rehearsal room, and down came the rain; lightning, thunder; and the noise couldn't have been worse. The room got darker, the sound of the water on the roof was deafening, and if any of the film footage is usable it will be a great surprise to me. If only they had come last week, when we were still in the middle of the heat-wave; the only noises were birds singing outside and the light quality was brilliant.

The public began to arrive as we finished; the people seem almost an intrusion! The real business goes on in rehearsals; life changes for us on the day of the final Dress Rehearsal and the fun is over.

We were talking today about the danger involved in Orfeo's attempts to look Euridice in the eyes, the very thing the gods have forbidden him to do if he is to bring his wife safely back from the Underworld. From time to time Peter has asked me to turn towards her so that the audience see me almost yielding to the temptation, but not quite. The extent of the head movement is difficult to get right because I must rely absolutely on the outside help of the producer to tell me when to stop. As we worked today, my head can move much nearer to Euridice's face than I imagine, because she is really already in my vision before I am told to stop. It is one of the rare moments when I cannot judge a move for myself, and it is a strange feeling for someone as instinctive as myself to stop turning my head. This is what rehearsals are for; testing the warmth of the water, deciding how far one can go.

One of the most exciting things for an audience is to watch performers taking risks; the high note for a voice; the almost impossible leap for a dancer; the level of an emotion for an actor; we must dare constantly.

When I was playing Penelope in *Ulysses* here, we used a ramp which extended out over the orchestra, and I would go right to the edge of it at certain moments. My doing so caused a tension in me, and in the audience, which raised the temperature of the moment.

Silence can also do this. There are points when everything ceases for a fraction of time; to judge the length of these silences is a great challenge, and they are as important as the music.

Sunday We lose track of weekends here. Sunday is an ordinary working
13 June day. A happy morning, doing dancing. Stuart thinks we're quick on the uptake and wants to give us even more! It *is* fun although hard work; nobody expects us to be dancers, so if we make even a mildly good shot at it, we feel a terrific sense of achievement. This afternoon I felt we had a breakthrough. In the moments when we get it 'right', i.e. *feel* the dramatic action through the mind, heart and solar plexus, instead of throwing our arms around and moving about, we begin to 'taste' the feel and these moments are becoming more frequent.

Rosenkavalier first performance was already well under way by the end of our rehearsal. It brings me up very sharply to be reminded that the whole idea of our work is for the public. It is easy to be so totally absorbed in our discoveries during rehearsal.

207

Monday 14 June We go, like school children, from music calls to dancing class to production rehearsals; to the corrections, the adaptations and the faltering steps forward; *just* like being at school.

There is no difference between days of the week, or between week and weekend: after work I am often not able even to take an evening walk, having been on my feet for so many hours, all I want to do is climb into a hot bath and then get into bed.

My balsa-wood lyre arrived this afternoon. It looks exactly like the heavy one; I'm not certain which of them I will choose; having carried the heavy one I slow up my movements with the new lyre which helps to counteract the lightness; so that has been one positive gain. My old lyre looks at me reproachfully from the side of the stage as if to say, 'What have I done?'

The conveyor belt feel has returned to the Opera House. We have now moved up one, from being 'new boys' we are 'gentlemen in waiting'; now *Rosenkavalier* is on, we are next and the *Don Giovanni* cast takes over from us at the end of the queue; their first night is after ours. Groups of people one saw daily disappear for good, since the singers just come in for their own performances. The *Don* cast are in their first stages, so we bump into them at break instead.

There is a great difference in the working atmosphere of this House. At Covent Garden and the Coliseum, the only place in either building common to all is the canteen. Here we have the beautiful Green Room where people read, snooze, or write letters, the wonderful gardens to walk in and the lake to look at. We visit each other and there is time to talk. Nevertheless Glyndebourne is the personification of introversion. People here don't believe anything is happening elsewhere, or if it is it can't be of real importance! One forgets, working here, that there is a world outside at all.

But I miss London. I miss my meetings, however infrequent, with a group of friends. Every so often four of us gather in a simple café in Hampstead to talk about things which interest us.

208

With Elisabeth Speiser

They are by far the most interesting conversations I ever have, and this year has made such indulgence impossible. Very soon I shall be able to see my friends again. I have not been free to attend a single Munster Trust audition either; I am usually very faithful in fulfilling my duties as a Trustee and enjoy not only the opportunity to hear young musicians and help them financially, but spending a day with other colleagues on the Trust. It is an aspect of my life which is hard to fit in, but infinitely worthwhile.

The last opera stretches on to the middle of August; because after the performances are over we have the Promenade concert, (a semi-staged version), then we record it, and make a television film of it.

Only after that can I look forward to a short holiday and the prospect of celebrating our silver wedding in September. When the season begins, the new régime comes into force and my life will be properly spaced; there will be adequate time between each engagement, time to savour the friends I want to see and the things I want to do.

People are already asking me to sing concert performances of opera in the future. Although I agreed a long time ago to do *Damnation of Faust* with the LSO next winter, and *Dido and Aeneas* at the King's Lynn Festival during the summer of 1983, I shall not make a habit of transferring roles I would normally have played on stage onto the concert platform. The two operas I have just mentioned take to concert performances particularly well, but to tackle something like Donizetti's *Parisina* which was suggested recently, sounds alarmingly like the thin end of the wedge; I have no intention of falling into that particular trap. Judging by all the letters which still keep arriving, wishing me well in my 'retirement', I shall meet the remark, 'But we thought you had retired from singing' many times during the immediate future engagements!

Another reaction I've been getting lately from opera fans about my quitting the stage is a quizzical look, then – 'You don't *really* mean it, do you?' The answer is 'Yes – I really *do*!'   I know performers who genuinely do enjoy performing; they start with this valuable attitude and perhaps for them it could be very hard to stop. Having eaten, breathed, and slept music for many, many years, total dedication to one aspect of life now seems unnecessary to me, grateful though I am and always will be to my profession and those involved with it. But there is a great big beautiful world out there which doesn't care a fig about performance, and I want to explore it before it's too late. Music is a jealous mistress; I have given her everything I have for as long as I can remember. When she gets her hands on you, you're finished, and what I'm doing now is trying to persuade her to loosen her grip – just a little!

Tuesday
15 June   My father went home this morning. In the theatre all day, our first complete one; we had scenery and electrical equipment, which meant trees going on and off, rocks appearing and disappearing, and gods flying up and down. Poor Amor (Elizabeth Gale) is stuck up on apparatus, standing motionless, through most of the opera. She was extremely brave about it, even when the man manipulating her movements began to get cocky during the late afternoon and whizzed her up and down at an alarming rate; she is belted securely to a steel post but has to stand on a tiny platform with nothing in front to hold on to. Like travelling in a lift without any sides!

The set looks marvellous, strong, simple; today we felt like a real opera. After lunch I actually had a moment in which to go and sit in my dressing room while I waited for my next call to the stage. It was relatively peaceful, the window open, the chintz curtains moving in the breeze, and outside the mulberry tree to look at.

Jean Mallandaine came over to supper when we finished at 6 p.m. Jeanie is a brilliant musician on the staff here, but is at

211

Houston Opera for most of the year, where she is Head of Music Staff. She has been a friend for years and like so many of our colleagues we don't see enough of her. She was extremely kind to Keith during the run of *Calisto*, taking him into the orchestra pit every night and allowing him to see the opera sitting by her side. She told me a day or two ago that she used to let Keith sound the A on her harpsichord for the orchestra to tune to; this became quite a ritual and caused great amusement to the band; the leader treated Keith like one of the boys. Apparently one night Ray came into the pit after the interval and raised the orchestra to take the customary applause; up got Keith with the others, obviously thinking he deserved some applause too! He doesn't think he'll be able to manage the job this year because our piano at home has been away for overhaul and he's forgotten just where A is on the keyboard!

The war in the Falklands is at an end. Thank God.

Now we have the difficult job of keeping the peace so many lost lives have paid for.

Wednesday   Another long hard morning on stage. We are all carefully
16 June   treading our way as individuals; in a few days we shall be a unit. Euridice and I had our costumes on. Mine feels so good I forgot it *was* a costume; light, comfortable, it is like a second skin. No shoes or wigs yet. I have been wearing my old *Calisto* sandals; what memories they bring back!

When standing becomes unbearable, I lie down flat on the stage, waiting. It is important for us all to be very patient; there is a lot of hanging around involved while we try to master difficult manoeuvres. After lunch we practised alone, Elisabeth and I, with Stuart. We have a tricky move when the confrontation comes. She walks towards me down the ramp and I have to catch her as she dies and place her on the floor; Stuart

212

can tell us exactly what to do with our feet and how to balance our weight so that we don't fall off the stage in a heap at Ray's feet! What a catastrophe that would be! Later, as I left, I went into the ladies' number one dressing room to have a few words with Elizabeth (Harwood) who was sitting at the dressing-table, getting her make-up on for her role as the Marschallin. I watched her for a while as we talked. She has always been a beautiful woman; now, in her forties, with the years of her life and her experience as a wife, mother and singer, written across her face, she is even more so, and it is because of her kindness and loving qualities as a human being.

Peter has gone to Greece for a couple of days, to tuck away the cast of the *Oresteia* safely into their temporary abode at Epidaurus. I asked him to give the boys a message, and to say how much their playing had helped me with Orfeo. We have to try to communicate with our audience without masks as directly, simply, and honestly as they did with them.

The audience began to arrive soon after we had finished lunch. It is always a shock to see them. I have been wondering why the situation here seems somehow 'unreal'? I think it is because Glyndebourne's prime function is as a womb, a place of gestation, or a Mother image. Of course the audience comes in to share and the touring company goes out into the highways and by-ways, but that isn't quite the same.

What happens here is unusual work, rare because there is time to do it properly. People specifically come here to work with each other, making sacrifices to do so; there is creativity at a high level and exciting things happen. It is opera at its best, and it is wonderful for youngsters like the members of the chorus to see all this at the outset of their careers. But Glyndebourne is not a true reflection of the way the world of opera works. Because the House is so tiny and the stage in proportion so large, we play together in an intimate way; and as it is Festival Opera it is of a limited duration. In its early days Glyndebourne set a standard

213

which the rest of the country then strove to equal. We go away from here having experienced theatre in ideal conditions, in order to take those ideals and standards elsewhere, just as we took them in different ways from Aldeburgh, through the influence of Ben (Britten) and Peter (Pears).

The vague feeling of intrusion I get when the audience arrives stems, I believe, from the fact that here they do not seem our first concern. The audience, for the most part, comes for the total Glyndebourne experience, not primarily for the music; we, the players, are concerned with the quality of the work and opportunities for learning. This may sound like heresy and of course it is, because as performers our first concern should undoubtedly *be* the people who come to hear us. It *is* really!

Glyndebourne has been criticised for its exclusivity, for the small number of people it actually serves. The touring company, which provides invaluable opportunities for the younger musicians to try their wings, helps to redress this balance as do the Promenade Concert appearances, the recordings, and television recordings of our work. But if one thinks of Glyndebourne as a matrix, the idea falls into place. A birthplace must have peace, adequate time, protection from the outside world. Anyone who knows the operatic scene in this country knows what Glyndebourne's contribution has been, and is today. Certain places, just like certain people, are power-houses, centres from which radiations come, affecting levels of achievement far beyond their own boundaries. They have to be 'special' or 'exclusive' because of the nature of their task. As such a centre, Glyndebourne needs no justification. It succeeds totally.

Thursday We have crawled along this morning. It is time usefully spent,
17 June ironing out practical problems. The children responsible for bringing on the flame to be extinguished on Euridice's grave are

214

very tiny, and we had to take them over and over this difficult move.

Whenever I am not needed, I use the opportunity to relax and I stretch full out to save energy. These days before we start complete runs can be depleting, and I must harbour my resources. Orfeo himself grows more and more human, less and less a 'god' in my own mind. He becomes ever more simple and natural. Perhaps the great heroic qualities which he must possess are easier to share through the frail vessel of an ordinary man, and more deeply touching too.

This afternoon we had the orchestra for the first time. It is so good to hear the score in all its glory. It is utterly different; a rich carpet of sound under us.

Friday 18 June Guus Mostart, Peter's talented associate producer, has worked with us, patiently, all day, taking us forward, repeating this morning the difficult and complicated procedure at the end of the opera; in the afternoon, more dancing steps to learn.

Tomorrow, when we have the orchestra for the first time for a stage rehearsal, we will see a reversal of the emphasis; up to now we have concentrated on memorising moves, getting to grips with the psychology of the characterisation, next the musical side will take precedence until problems of balance are sorted out. What one hopes will then emerge is an equality between the two; often this is not achieved by first night. The pressure of a first night can easily delay a finely balanced production because it is an abnormal event. When the run settles down we shall see an organic growth taking place, but usually only the performers see this happen. Most people who see the opera will do so once, and therefore can only understand a small fraction of its actual life. First nights are births. Last nights are deaths. The truth about our efforts is a total of these two events, plus all the moments in between.

215

Yesterday as I made a move on stage I had that strange feeling most of us have at some time or another, that I had been in the same place, making the same move before. It is an odd experience.

Saturday
19 June   Peter is back with us: he had left Athens at 4 a.m. but arrived looking amazingly fresh after a night without sleep, delighted by the National's triumph in Epidaurus. He told me how thrilled with the perfect acoustics the cast had been.

Orchestra and stage rehearsal today; everything still feels very disjointed. My boots arrived this morning – at last. I think they will be alright; I intend to wear them around the flat to break them in, they need a small adjustment to the ankle which isn't as pliable as it needs to be. I don't suppose John Bury had anticipated my following in the footsteps of Margot Fonteyn!

Every time I do the 'Hades' scene with the chorus there is another extraordinary costume to startle the wits; from close quarters the weird animal shapes and grotesque masks completely disguise my friends in the chorus. I can't tell who anybody is any more!

We worked away at balance problems until lunch, and then back to the 'dance floor' until 6 p.m. when I went to change for the first act of *Rosenkavalier*, feeling filthy, dusty, untidy, and totally unlike a proper Glyndebourner! Since I was tucked away in a corner of the press box it didn't matter in the least and I just got to my seat in time, having said to Simon Rattle as he dashed past, 'Hold the curtain until I get to the box!'

I was grateful for the darkened theatre; for most of the first act I sat unable to stop tears from pouring down my face. To see the Marschallin played is always a touching and nostalgic experience, especially for women, but when the character above all is sung by a colleague who is also a dearly loved friend, then the circumstances are almost unbearable. Elizabeth, with her

216

impeccable German, perfectly phrased Strauss, her inner sweetness, her beauty, the dignity of her person and the soaring, creamy voice, was deeply moving. I felt her interpretation significant in two ways; for her, personally, at this moment in her life and career, and then for myself. In all these months since the season began, I have never felt a moment of regret for the decision I have made; I still do not, but sitting there at the back of the box, watching my friend, I felt deep grief. There is no shame at feeling grief at parting; it is a natural emotion, and it swept over me in painful waves as I listened, aware of my years as a theatre person, of my memories, my colleagues. The final nights at Covent Garden and the Coliseum were full of glory. I have every hope that the last night here at Glyndebourne will be the same; my own real 'goodbye' to the stage was being said tonight in my own heart, there in the press box, and the actual words of that 'good-bye' were being sung on the stage by my friend. It seemed planned in some remarkable way that I should feel as I did, sitting quite alone (there were strangers in the box with me, thank goodness), sharing the moment with Elizabeth who was quite unaware of her part in the proceedings. After all these months I now fully understand what I have done. Apollo has reached out and branded me for daring to walk away from the profession instead of waiting to be cast aside, but in the pain of understanding what I have willingly given up and in my total acceptance of it, I have paid in full my debt to the theatre. The scales are even. I am handing back the power lent to me, and in so doing am burned. It is an honourable wound.

Sunday
20 June
A glorious day and I am free for all of it. We took a picnic lunch and drove through heavenly lanes to find a small hotel which I had read about. When we come back to televise *Orfeo* the flat won't be available so we need somewhere quiet and comfortable. It was all I had hoped and more, so we saw a room and booked it

for August. Lunched in an idyllic spot. Oh! England on a perfect summer day! All this green and the sun as well. Waist-high in cow-parsley, bracken and foxgloves we wrote our family letters, read the Sunday papers, and snoozed. Then a long walk, longer than we anticipated because we got lost. I have a compass tucked away in my solar plexus and on the rare occasions Keith takes a wrong turning late at night coming back from a concert, and I am fast asleep in the car, I wake up immediately and say, 'This doesn't feel right.' My instinct has been proved correct a number of times over the years and is a joke between us. But today, no vibes; I am still feeling shattered by my experiences of yesterday, perhaps my emotions need to be calm for my inner pathfinder to work. It didn't matter; we enjoyed the countryside so much.

My poor feet are covered in blisters – all that dancing with my new boots on, no doubt!

We entertained some colleagues this evening at a small restaurant nearby, and then they all came back here for coffee. Just the right ending to a perfect day.

Monday
21 June
The longest day – in many senses of the word!

In every production there is a lowest point. That was today. We were in the theatre, dressed and made up ready for our first orchestral run-through at 2.30. My wig is so natural, everybody thinks it is my own hair! Boots, now modified, are comfortable and my only problem is my long cotton leggings which kept sinking down and wrapping themselves around my ankles. I slipped out front whenever I could (which was for about four minutes during the entire day) to glimpse the set, now lighted, and the costumes; what I saw was magical. All went well until the final act which we expected to prove difficult; it involves everyone and many people on a stage always cause problems.

218

At the break we went into the courtyard for some welcome sun and air, then at 7 p.m. back into the theatre.

As the evening wore on the danger grew. After a tiring, frustrating day, with many things still to get right, tempers usually ignite quickly. This is the moment when the prima donna throws herself on the floor, kicks, screams, and announces she's going home. The producer flings up his hands in despair, the designer throttles the head of the wardrobe department, the orchestra and chorus decide to strike, and the conductor feels like sacking the lot of us to start again from scratch!

But although we were all dog-tired, the atmosphere in the theatre was calm, no voice was raised, no harsh words were said. I suppose everyone realised that getting angry wastes precious energy and we didn't have any of that to spare. The pressures caused by extreme fatigue and the complications caused by strange costumes bring us to the point of despair. A good night's sleep usually solves this and tomorrow morning the world will look different again.

Wednesday *23 June* The last three days have merged into one. I have eaten, walked around, worked in a sort of horrific daze and a rather frightening pattern has emerged. The rehearsals have caused me no difficulty at all, and for as long as I've needed to, I have been able to draw on an amazing, unfailing source of energy, such as I have never before known; I have had at my command an endless supply of patience and physical stamina during the time we have been in the theatre, and particularly in this final week when everything becomes more pressured. On getting into the flat I have washed off the filth from the stage, climbed into bed and waited for sleep to come. And waited; because sleep has *not* come. I have lain awake, wide, wide awake, with the score endlessly playing over and over in my head like some macabre record; sometimes sleeping but always fitfully, and never later

219

than 6.30 a.m. Up, breakfast, and into the theatre earlier and earlier, today by 9 a.m.

I cannot imagine why my body plays me so false at the very time when I need deep sleep so badly to repair the strain of work. This strange 'overdrive' I'm in is a highly un-natural state and worries me. If I don't get back to normal I must have some help; I feel just like the spring of a clock which is being wound up tighter and tighter. I have been using every available moment to lie flat on my back stretched out on the working ramp, and now the chorus are beginning to think it's a good idea and they lie down too! So do the dancers. Somebody called out yesterday, 'Where's Jan?' and up I rose out of a heap of tangled bodies, chorus in their 'Furies' costumes, dancers in their furry animal ones; some funny conversations take place down there on the floor!

These last hours before a new production goes on are inevitably traumatic; the final scene is causing a lot of trouble, but today when we had been in the theatre from 9 a.m. until 7 p.m. much of the opera felt well on the way, with moments of sheer magic.

The film team took over at the end of the rehearsal and we did the famous lament 'Che farò', which Bob wants to include in our film. We were so well into our work after the long day that we only needed one take and it was in the bag.

My leggings are still falling around my ankles. I seem to spend all my time hitching them up; my shoes have stretched and must have a different fastening made, thank goodness they arrived in time for this to happen before the public Dress Rehearsal. My wig has to be cut shorter, I look too much like a girl, and my dagger belt curls over. Make-up is also too heavy for this tiny House; one doesn't need anything stronger than the usual evening make-up for concerts. There should really be a free day tomorrow but we need more work on the final scene, so principals are called.

220

Production notes at 10.30 and a slow thorough discussion with Peter and Ray about what went wrong yesterday and why. This is our last chance to talk, modify or change; this day is one I always dread because tomorrow we hand over the piece, lock, stock, and barrel to the 'customers'. From now on it's theirs, not ours, however hard I try to persuade myself that Glyndebourne is different, in this respect. Of course it *isn't*. The point of performing is to perform and now we cease to play it for ourselves. There is a terrible pain in this fact too; I will never again take part in weeks like those just drawing to a close, where colleagues experiment, exchange ideas, and create something beautiful.

This is a small cast and the unit has therefore had an intimacy: morning after morning we have gathered on the rehearsal stage with the big doors and the sun pouring through, to indulge in this absorbing, fascinating, wonderful world. Watching the audience arrive for another opera has made the people unreal. Tomorrow, they arrive for us.

I shall no longer go into the Opera House every day, just for my own performances; I shall miss feeling I belong to a group because, shut away in our dressing rooms, one only meets people actually on stage. As my performances are every other day for the most part, I shall have to husband my resources and take care not to speak much on my days off.

The train strike is making life difficult for everyone, and Keith is driving home to fetch my father tomorrow, so we will be a family again. This afternoon we hung around waiting for some new props to arrive and then worked very hard trying to perfect the most difficult manoeuvre in the opera – but we could only try it out with the dancers, since the chorus wasn't called in.

This role is gradually twining itself around my heart; the battle of opposites, with which it is so deeply involved, between life and death, heaven and hell, light and dark, courage and fear, bears curious witness to the battle raging between Apollo, god of

With Raymond Leppard, Peter Hall and Elisabeth Speiser

light, reason, individuality, and his half-brother Dionysus, who represents instinct, chaos, mass hysteria.

If only we could get the proper balance between the two gods within and find the right proportion of individual, reasonable behaviour supported by instinct and passion, we would be supermen, but the history of this struggle and our failure to meet it is the history of the human race.

It seems fitting that the last role I shall ever play on a stage is Orfeo. My own struggles to come to terms with my art and public versus private life, are focused at this moment in a very special way. Usually, characters one plays contain facets of one's own personality, but they are still 'other people', although for me quite real in themselves. Orfeo is on every level myself, a meeting point for the art of singing, a symbol of my profession, a representative of impersonal forces in the widest possible sense and also of myself as a human being.

Painful though the battle is, it means one thing – Life – and when it ceases to rage we might as well lie down and die.

This theme runs through the entire Glyndebourne season. The operas all speak of different aspects of love, and the various ways in which the operatic characters meet the challenges presented. In a very real sense the Orphic myth, the celebration of the mysteries, is concerned with love and life and death; the triumph, in Gluck's score, is of love over death; *Love for Three Oranges* speaks for love in its less serious aspect; *The Barber of Seville* for romantic love prior to marriage; *Rosenkavalier* of that particularly poignant moment when a mature woman relinquishes her much younger lover to a young girl; *Don Giovanni* of lust. It would be a fascinating experience to see each of the operas presented here on consecutive nights!

Friday Public Dress Rehearsal. Keith left for London early. Jean came
25 June over for coffee and we talked for a while before going to the

223

Opera House together in her car, she to lunch with an American friend, I to my dressing room to practise and to prepare my table; my tapestry cloth was used for the first time here; the dressing-table is a long, long shelf, and it looks extremely bare and hard; once my fabric, stained with powder, wig glue, and a hundred other things which never come out in the wash, is laid over the expanse, the room becomes mine. I put out everything I needed; Elizabeth had left me some garden flowers in a pot (bless her) from the night before. Then I went into the canteen at 1.30 for my usual salad; the place was packed; it shows just how good the food is this year.

At 2.15 the cast met in one of the rehearsal rooms; we were to run over the new cuts made yesterday in the last scene which the chorus hadn't tried out, so for three-quarters of an hour we went over the sections involved. A short final pep-talk from Peter and then onto the stage to repeat the same last, difficult scene in the proper place.

At 3.40 we were free to go; the audience had already begun to arrive. To me, it seemed just like a first night; at the end of these weeks of total concentration, hard physical work, and lack of sleep, my nerves were at breaking point. During the time left before curtain up I sat getting ready, trying, unsuccessfully, to conquer them; Peter came in to talk. He told me how completely he understands my decision to stop this terrifying drain on every single resource; he has seen many performers in the state I was in just then, who after years of performing, simply cannot take the punishment any longer. He said it all lies in the difference between those who watch the process and those who actually do it. He is right.

Curtain up; pouring rain; out there in the dark of the auditorium real people to be communicated with: I couldn't see them, of course, I never do, because of my bad eyesight, but the real reason is that one sees with the mind and my mind is full of the score and what I'm doing; there isn't room for anything else.

224

Although one appears to be looking at an audience, if one's concentration is as it should be, 'seeing' them in the normal sense of the word is impossible.

We made a great deal of magic today, helped by the warm vibes of colleagues sitting watching us – including a boxful of 'Rosenkavaliers' who all came round for a hug afterwards, many friends, and some family; then to the organ room for discussion.

I decided to get cleaned up at home so drove back in my make-up.

I haven't had the slightest sensation of time passing, today. It was a shock to realise that the day was over – 9.30 p.m. and the whole landscape covered in a soft, silvery blue mist, with tree tops sticking out of it like the weird landscape of a country I had never seen before, surrounded by a fabulous, gentle, shell-pink sky. Nature, exhausted by the furies of heavy rain, had put on colours of the utmost fragility, looking exactly as I felt.

Sunday
27 June
My father and I had a walk by the sea; the wind was strong but warm and as we went I told him what *Orfeo* was about. He likes *me* to tell him in my own words what I'm doing up there – it seems more real to him than a synopsis in a programme. It is a simple matter to speak the outline of this extremely simple story.

The utter turmoil and desolation which has assailed me during these weeks of rehearsing it is far from simple, and only I can ever know what this desperate journey of Orfeo's has done to me; in the process of entering Hades and conquering the Furies, in the test of will and discipline involved in bringing Euridice back from the dead and obeying the god's demand not to look at her, Orfeo fails. The gods know the fatal weakness in all of us and choose the very thing they know we cannot do. Of course Orfeo fails the test. Of course everybody does. The myth says Euridice stays dead; I think this is a true picture of the situation. Gluck's

225

happy ending is fine for theatre
but in real life the only
positive factor seems to be
the way we accept our
defeat, the way we accept
our 'death'; to summon up
the courage and step forward
into the unknown, while
knowing one is totally helpless,
totally at the mercy of life, is
Man's destiny and glory.
I thank God for the faith
which tells me that somewhere
out there in the dark an
ultimate goal is to be found
which is worth the suffering.
As yet I have not found it,
but I do have my small
number of priceless friends
who, in my direst moments,
hold out their hands to me in
love. I certainly don't deserve
them, but I do believe that
the quality of friendship
which it is my privilege to
enjoy, is perhaps the most
beautiful relationship human
beings can know. It is 'caritas',
St Paul's 'charity', and it is one
of the blessings given to those
who are treading the same path.
   All the turmoil, agony
and pain of *Orfeo* is
now inside me, and

226

it is ready to be given out to other people; only just. Until today, his journey has overwhelmed me; now I am able to stand aside from it, and all the emotions which the character and the score have let loose in me can be channelled into the proper source – our performances. We drove to the theatre; the evening would be fine.

My dressing room a bower of flowers, cards, presents and a stream of people wishing me well.

From the moment the curtain rose until it came down again I was filled with a tremendous calm, the long interval went very quickly. Our final scene which had caused us so much trouble went off without a hitch and at the end, that first night audience left us in no doubt at all what their feelings about the evening had been. They went wild, and Peter and Ray were both beaming with delight. The Christies gave a splendid party in their end of the lovely house, and when at last I was clean and tidy I joined them all. There is nothing like the feeling one has at the end of a job well done; to know that the work of so many people, so many hours, has been justified, and that we haven't let anyone down. The room was filled with distinguished guests, staff, wives, friends, a really special occasion. We drove back to London afterwards to be home for twenty-four hours; the house was glad to see us; I felt it as soon as I walked through the front door.

There were actors in the audience tonight and Trevor Nunn from the R.S.C. They came round to see me. I find it difficult to believe, but I suppose I must, that my world does for actors what theirs does for me. When they come to tell me what a performance has meant and what my own acting has meant, my cup is full. They are moments to treasure, and I do. The other highlight of the day was to find among the many kind messages on my dressing-table a lovely card from the chorus. They had all signed it, and had put 'From your chorus'; that one word *your* was of such significance to me. During these weeks my two Elizabeths, Gale and Speiser, Amor and Euridice, have

228

proved delightful colleagues. We have been a happy team. With the chorus, since that magical moment on the first day when we began to touch each other's hands, I have felt a bond. To see that they signed their message to me in this particular way was of the deepest significance. They belong, of course, first to themselves, then to Glyndebourne, to their fantastic Chorus Master, Jane Glover, and to their conductors and producers for whom they work, but on *Orfeo* nights they belong to me.

Tuesday 29 June   Strange to be at home, but lovely too. In spite of very heavy showers we got all the grass cut, but with the boxes off – so the garden looks as though we're about to make hay.

A busy editing session on Monday evening when much useful work was done and I was able to see the actual book jacket; another exciting landmark in the process.

This evening after preparing the house as much as we could for guests who will be using it while we are away, we packed our tennis togs, unused for years, and drove back to Brighton – a marvellous, golden evening. Our unforgettably beautiful journeys to and from Sussex are an important part of the entire season. On our arrival we quickly unpacked and then went for a long walk by the sea-shore. I am now sleeping, long and deeply. It is wonderful to sleep – a thing we take so completely for granted when it happens naturally, but which assumes frightening proportions when it doesn't come easily.

Wednesday 30 June   A lovely day, cool but fine. Second performance – a dangerous day. Now that our child is born, we have to nurture it and watch it grow. I have never known the final week of rehearsal go easily; the birth pangs are always painful and traumatic. This is perhaps why first nights have a unique tension – they are the culmination of the process and it is understandable that there should be an

229

atmosphere in the theatre and amongst the performers which is there only at that particular moment. When we no longer have adrenalin flow, caused by this process, the hard work begins – trying to make technique look natural so that each audience will feel we are playing it for the first time, for them!

Thursday
1 July

Tennis today with Jean, and Bernard Haitink, who is madly keen to play. The blighters stole a march on us and got out onto the court at 8.30 a.m. to practise. By the time we had anxiously inspected the sky and driven over to Glyndebourne for a short try-out ourselves, it was lunch time so we had a light salad in the canteen. At 2 p.m. the great game began. Jean plays a lot in Houston but the three of us hadn't touched a tennis racquet in years; it's rather like riding a bicycle – you never really forget, and although we weren't wildly accurate, we looked alright doing it! Keith and I, convinced we would get slaughtered, put up a decent fight and I was enjoying myself so much just being there in the air, playing a game I love, with extremely pleasant companions.

After about an hour I suddenly felt strange, and in a few minutes had to leave the court; the unbelievable had happened and my allergy, like a thunderbolt, struck me down. A doctor was called; Mary Christie held my head while I was violently sick, and I felt the familiar, ghastly symptoms beginning, fighting for breath, as my face swelled up. The doctor arrived in record time and injected me with piriton, and after a little while Keith took me home. The anti-histamine made me extremely drowsy and I slept for the rest of the day.

Friday
2 July

My understudy, Carolyn Watkinson, is standing by in the theatre this evening which relieves my mind a great deal. By the time I leave, mid-afternoon, I have been in bed for twenty-four hours and feel extremely weak but rested. On the way, I call at the surgery, and Dr. Carter gives me a shot of vitamin B to try and boost my energy.

The day is scorching and the theatre very claustrophobic.

Everybody very concerned, and kind Carolyn is absolutely prepared and ready to go on, but she understands that I have to try and perform if I possibly can. By some miracle (and I wish I knew exactly why) my face has gone back almost to normal which is a great relief; the worst swelling was in the throat membranes and it has been very difficult to swallow, but as I warm up, the voice begins to sound free; I manage to survive until the dinner interval, and can then stretch out on my divan.

During the second part of the evening my body obeys me more easily; the habit of imposing my will and making myself perform under less than ideal circumstances asserts itself more strongly, and I summon up energy from somewhere.

Everyone says it is impossible to tell I'm under par in any way and I am thankful for that. Even more thankful to get home and sleep.

Saturday
3 July

I am paying today for what I forced myself to do yesterday as I knew I would. We had to go into the Opera House for an interview, and afterwards Keith and I walked round the lake. At least, we walked halfway there, because I simply could not manage the distance. When I think of the enormous amount of energy I have had at my disposal during the weeks of rehearsal, it is laughable that I can't walk even such a short way. But today, I don't have to force myself to do anything and I decide to listen to what my body is telling me. We walk back to the house slowly and go up to Moran Caplat's room to see the drawing of the platform set up for the Promenade Concert of *Orfeo*, which is his special 'baby', and we talk usefully about the project. Lunch in the canteen, then home, and I am able again to sleep.

231

This place is really the most extraordinary microcosm. In what other opera house in the world could one be surrounded by children, dogs, tiny kittens, people playing tennis, the scent of marvellous flowers, glimpses of a lake covered in water lilies, the downs surrounding it all, and like the bass section of a great orchestra holding the deep harmony of a symphony, the sound of *Don Giovanni* rehearsals going on in the theatre; our *raison d'etre* wrapped up in so many facets of every-day life. No wonder the music here is special. So are the people who work here. They have achieved a remarkable thing, the highest possible professional standards, but instead of the rat race such standards usually imply, the work is done near a small town surrounded by beautiful countryside. The work seems to be a natural outcome of the place.

Sunday Keith and I took the same route by the sea that my father and I
4 July walked last Sunday. Only seven days ago but it feels like years.

During the interview with Edward Greenfield yesterday, the question of the validity of the first act aria 'Addio miei sospiri' cropped up. Some people don't think it should be there. I explained my view of the situation, which is simple and reasonable.

The opera is often done in the way which makes Orfeo's last remark 'Assist me, then, gods. I accept the challenge', come at the end of a recitative; he sings about the effect his refusal to look at Euridice will have upon her and about his fears for her reaction.

If there is no 'bridge', psychologically, between his anxious state of mind and his confrontation with the Furies, there is no way he could enter that hell and survive. Many primitive tribes employ the trick of the war-dance to gear themselves up for a difficult task or a battle. Orfeo, too, needs precisely the same help to prepare him for the next stage of the journey – so does the

232

Act III, with Elisabeth Speiser

audience, and this aria fulfils this
need exactly. Orfeo gets up his
courage, the audience hears a
change of mood, and they are both
then ready to brave the Underworld.
The inclusion of this aria is, in
my view, totally justified. Musically
speaking, it gives a true picture of
human experience, light and shade,
happiness and gloom, one always
precedes the other and each gains
from the other.

It is the same with the scene after
the Furies, when lovely little animals
approach Orfeo and he responds
to them; the atmosphere is
lightened a little by the touching
movements of the acrobats and
dancers, and this again forms a
'bridge' leading so naturally and
gracefully into the next section,
which involves Euridice and the
Blessed Spirits.

When I get back to my dressing
room for the interval, Ruth, my
dresser, lights my sandal-wood
candle and when I am changed
into a dressing-gown I lean out of
the window to listen to the wind
playing in the leaves of the
mulberry tree, close enough to touch.
I watch the shadows sharpen the
outlines of the distant shapes in the
garden. It is sheer delight.

234

With
Elizabeth Gale

Heaven is a leafy Sussex lane in hot sunshine, a picnic tea, books to read while drinking it, a snooze afterwards, undisturbed by traffic; only the sounds of the breeze in the tree-tops, bird-song and the odd dog barking in the distance. It is a day spent doing the things one enjoys most and includes dinner with friends to round it off; such a day sandwiched between performances which now come thick and fast, is a restoring process.

I wonder if it is the approach of middle-age which teaches sharper enjoyment? Certainly I find I enjoy everything more and more, particularly natural events, the changing seasons, or the colours of the sky; I would not have gained such pleasure fifteen years ago, as I did today from watching butterflies tumbling over each other in the hedge-bottom; I would not have made time to do such a thing. In fact, until quite recently time has been only for music, for work, for recovery from work.

Suddenly, my life is enriched with theatre, friendships of great importance, a deeper need of family, of moments in which to stand and wonder. If there is to be more of this in the coming years, give me middle-age every time!

Retirement, even a partial one, seems to imply standing back – a desire to create space around oneself so that one can look at life properly. It doesn't mean opting out, it probably means opting *in* if my own experience is much to go by. I feel as though I am re-joining the world in one sense, and in another claiming for myself a privacy, a silence which I badly need and undoubtedly deserve after so many years of outpouring.

It is a marvel how one can feel so replenished by the touch of a child's hand, or the feel of an animal's fur, or the overwhelming joy of a beautiful day.

Nevertheless, I still have to bring myself back to reality and start thinking about events which happen immediately after my Glyndebourne season is over. I go up to Manchester to rehearse *Das Lied* with the Hallé and Jimmy Loughran; we have not done this piece together for some years, but I know it will be as

237

exciting and enjoyable as the performance of *Nuits d'Été* which we did last October and which was one of the best I've ever done, thanks to him; he is a superb singer's conductor. We are to perform at the King's Lynn Festival, where for three years I am Artistic Co-Director. This responsibility ends next year, and it has been both illuminating and interesting to experience the business from the other side of the fence.

I am also preparing items for recital programmes next season – Brahms is wafting through my head along with Gluck.

Tuesday
6 July It is touching to see the expression on the faces of many people who come back-stage after *Orfeo*; *I* am moved to see how moved *they* are. Those who are reached by it are obviously affected deeply. Our performance is one unified event. For the audience it is hundreds of different performances. Each person grasps it in their own unique way; they look at it with their eyes, their understanding, and their heart. What they see is what they are. Someone will come into a theatre or concert hall in a certain frame of mind, in a specific mood, perhaps a negative one. For him, the performance, coloured by his thoughts and feelings, will perhaps 'fail' in some way. The failure is his.

Another person will arrive, with an open heart, a joyful state of mind; for him we will be positive. We will make him feel we have added to his joy. For him we are 'successful'. That success is also his.

Someone else bowed down with grief may find solace. For such a person our performance will be a 'healing'. The performance is exactly the same but to each person watching it, the truth of it is a truth multiplied by as many different facets as there are people in the building. This is one reason why it is so dangerous to pay undue attention to, or allow oneself to be influenced by, the opinion of another, either word of mouth or reading a newspaper

or magazine. The power of art is a person-to-person communication. It is meant for one ear, one heart at a time; one's
own. What is received is unique, and cannot be got vicariously
from listening to the remarks or opinions of others. One must
drink at the life-giving fountain for oneself. What is tasted there
depends upon the individual.

For us, the performers, another sort of life-and-death struggle
is going on. Our concern is how well we have prepared ourselves
to do the job, mentally, physically, spiritually. Only we can know
this and even then, partially; all we can do is try our best at a
particular moment, but it must be the best, nothing less. After
that, the result is not our concern.

I wrote on a piece of paper and stuck over my dressing-table
mirror the following phrase by A.E. I look at it long and hard
before I go out onto the stage. It reads: 'My friend, a man's
success or failure is always within his own soul.'

Wednesday
7 July
We are all scattered about the countryside in our various rented
places. Since Keith had to be up in London, I spent the day with
Elisabeth Speiser who must surely have the most beautiful
house in the district, a coach house standing in a famous garden
with a private walled garden of its own. Imagine a perfect
English summer's day, old beams, low ceilings, a dream cottage,
covered in climbing roses, and honeysuckle, enjoying views of a
beautiful manor house, a mediaeval dovecote and gentle wooded
hills. To spend time in such a spot with such a colleague is
recovery indeed. Elisabeth and I found, to our mutual delight,
that we enjoyed reading the same books; she has also travelled
her own private interior journey during her exploration of
Euridice, and the opera has been for her, as for me, an experience
on many levels.

We had an idyllic day; her husband and daughter arrive on
Sunday and Carolyn Watkinson, my understudy, who has been

239

sharing the house with her didn't return until early evening. Carolyn will do a number of performances of *Orfeo* with the touring company in the autumn, and I am determined to catch one of them somewhere en route, since she is an enormously gifted singer and it will be so interesting to see her do 'my' role. She is, as yet, unmarried. The two girls represent different ways of dealing with a performer's life; one is married and has the responsibility of children plus a career. The other without husband or children, just the job to think about. I stand in the middle, having a home and husband but no children. All three ways are perfectly possible life styles; all three can work equally well. It depends entirely on the sort of person you are, and what you want from life. It is as well to be clear about this, and an interesting fact emerges, at least in my experience, talking to women in this profession. Those who begin a career and then opt out to concentrate on a family, never feel completely fulfilled by family life if it is at the total expense of their ambitions. They hanker after what might have been, in professional terms. It seems that the natural performer must, somewhere along the line, perform! I can't believe, standing where I do today, that a career alone is worth the price one pays in human terms. To my mind, the best all-round answer is a form of compromise, in other words to try and have everything! There's a price to pay for this too, in physical exhaustion; any working wife and mother knows that; but if one can possibly juggle with life as a performer, as wife, and as mother, then one's experience must be rich indeed.

Being childless doesn't bother me in the least. I suppose I'm not maternally minded, and you can't imagine what having and bringing up a child can possibly be like if you haven't tried it. On the other hand I do know with certainty that to have disobeyed my instincts to sing would have ruined my life in some deep way, and I would have been far happier unmarried but performing, than married and not performing. The whole scene for working

240

women has altered radically since I began; there is much more 'give and take' between couples and a greater understanding generally; even building societies actually give mortgages on a joint income. They didn't when we first applied for one twenty-five years ago!

In the evening we drove to Ray's for dinner; Keith arrived separately having called at home briefly, to see that everything was well there.

Altogether a perfect day.

Saturday In one week I shall be (figuratively speaking) boarding my little
10 July boat and sailing away into the blue, free of all care! It won't
happen quite like that (I go up to Manchester to rehearse for the
opening King's Lynn concert), but I do think there will be a real
crossing of a threshold in my mind and I am looking forward to
it.

We saw the public Dress Rehearsal of *Don Giovanni* yesterday
afternoon, a brilliant cast and production; the 'Don' is enough to
put you off men for the rest of your life. What stupid creatures we
women are; a man says a soft word to us and we fall like ninepins,
but he has such music to beguile the heart with; it's Mozart's
fault he is so irresistible. From the first orchestral entry, Haitink
had us spell-bound. Elizabeth Gale (our Amor) is Zerlina, and
has been working all hours this week doing *Orfeo* performances
as well; she told me she is sleeping badly, and had only an hour's
sleep on one particular night. Like the real 'pro' she is, her
performances of both Amor and Zerlina are a positive delight to
the ear and eye. No one would guess the physical and emotional
drain on her to see what a standard she produces on stage – and
with a small baby to care for as well. This is the attitude and the
approach to life and work that I admire so much. I went along to
see her afterwards feeling ill at ease and hesitant to be walking on
territory which doesn't belong to me, except on my own
performance days. It is perhaps hard to imagine how alien one's
own dressing room corridor feels, one's own room even, when
someone else is occupying it. After all these years, I would
expect to walk back-stage anywhere and feel thoroughly at home.
But when I myself am not singing, the sense of being an outsider
is totally overwhelming. I don't know why.

Friends from Nottingham are in our house this weekend.

243

It is good to think of them there. I am pleased that their visit to Glyndebourne should take place on yet another perfect Summer evening.

I come off-stage after the Hades scene, both for a breather and to have my person put to rights. The chorus really goes to town on my costume and my wig; they tear at me, put their hands over my face, pull me to my knees and try to steal my lyre. It's lovely! When we have finished I am glad to rest for a minute or two while my hair is re-combed, but tonight I walked along the corridor and out onto the staircase leading down into the garden.

The picnic baskets were marking the spot each group had chosen. I could hear the orchestra playing the opening bars of the Elysian Fields music and I stood looking at the garden, the surrounding meadows and the sky, breathing in the scent of tobacco plants as it wafted over. Each detail of the moment, visual and emotional, seemed sharply etched in my mind as I stood there. I was in the middle of my work and in the middle of all this beauty; I felt all around me the good-will and affection of my colleagues. I wonder what it is that makes us *aware*? I count it as one of my greatest blessings that I am aware of my good fortune as a person; the knowledge deepens every experience and makes each one more significant. I savoured the moment and then walked back inside, picked up my lyre, and returned to the Elysian Fields.

Monday
12 July
Another glowing performance. We are relaxing; Ray is drawing from the orchestra a sound which is rich and warm. He has such close contact with us, the distance between him and the edge of the stage is a matter of feet; by the time we arrive at the recording in the middle of August the piece will be firmly anchored. It always helps greatly when we record opera with performances under our belts.

I have never known a work to be quite *this* responsive to

audience reaction. We can feel so quickly the attitude of the people out there; each evening has never felt less than good, but sometimes there are just more 'reachable' people present than at others, and tonight the vibes were particularly strong.

Beautiful letters and flowers from strangers and friends. Peter (Pears), Donald Mitchell, and Isidor Caplan sent a marvellous bouquet and heart-warming message one evening last week, and as Isidor and his wife actually came to the performance, I was able to see them and get first hand news of Peter. The news was good; he was marvellous at the Aldeburgh Festival this year and has now gone on holiday. I do miss seeing him. Next year I shall be there, and part of it all again. The difference between Aldeburgh and Glyndebourne is enormous; they have one thing in common, each is a power focus, and as an integral part of my own experience both are precious, in different ways. They are like old, beloved friends, and as is often the case with one's friends, the differences are the reasons for the value one places upon them. It would be dull indeed if one's friends were all alike.

One of the most fortunate aspects of my early days was to be involved with quality, right from the start. It is obvious what influence Glyndebourne standards have had on my operatic career; the influence has been so deep that I have striven never to work on the stage in any other way. To a very great extent I have succeeded, even though in doing so I have strictly limited my stage work to places within the British Isles. I was right to do so, since I am not solely an opera singer.

Benjamin Britten and Peter Pears are largely responsible for the tremendous upsurge of quality in British performances and performers ever since World War II. The stamp of excellence they placed on those of us fortunate enough to work with them cannot be over-estimated; although it had nothing to do with actual working conditions, it had everything to do with an inner attitude, and the debt I owe those two wonderful men is incalculable. Most performers who went through the experience of Aldeburgh must have known this feeling of being burned at the sacred fire. We survived the ordeal or we did not; but if we did, we were always changed, and I feel I was changed for the better. Ben and Peter gave us standards which turned us from national to international performers and the alteration in status which British perfomers are now accorded, the respect we are unreservedly given all over the world, is due in large measure to them, and to the focus of energy they created in that tiny, beautiful corner of Suffolk. The days when England was regarded as an unmusical nation are over. Our performers and performances stand comparison with the best. Almost thirty years have passed since I began my training; I could not have chosen a more exciting time in which to pursue a career, or better colleagues with whom to make the journey.

The richness of the tapestry is incredible. It is still unfinished.

Tuesday *13 July* Another scorching day. I had offered to put myself at the disposal of the chorus, and suggested we should have a free discussion. They organised a wonderful picnic underneath the mulberry tree; we gathered there for lunch and talked together for almost two hours, enjoying the sunshine, the view, the food, and the companionship. They are splendid young people and they asked interesting questions about my personal life and about my attitude to work. Towards the end of the session, someone asked what I considered my role to be in the future.

At this moment, I don't know. What may emerge as I gradually curtail my performances on the concert platform is an unknown factor. I did not sit down and plan my career, neither do I intend to plan the rest of my life from now on. Accepting what has come to me has proved an entirely satisfactory situation, and I shall go on doing precisely that. Whatever does arrive, I imagine will appear to me as some sort of marvellous present, in that life will be more fun, more free from responsibility. I am not afraid of responsibility. I just think I have had more than my share of the burdens it imposes, and look forward to years ahead with a much more care-free attitude.

Some of the young people expressed mystification that I could give up opera when I can still do it! It is a mystery to me too, not why I can give it up, but how I can find myself doing so with the sense of joy and completeness I undoubtedly have. The only answer I can find is that my attitude proves to me conclusively that the decision is right for me.

We talked a lot about success and failure and how important it is to know oneself as unique, to know that the individuality of one's own voice and contribution sets each of us apart, and that because of this, envies, jealousies, have no part in our relations with other singers.

I spoke of the need to compromise, to come to terms with limitation, imposed either by the talent itself or by life's circumstances, which might cause pain. We can only be what we are; we cannot change what we have been given, only develop it to the utmost; it is in the striving we find fulfilment, not in the actual size of the talent itself.

I tried to be as honest with them as I possibly could and I told them what a special time this has been for me, working, communicating, making magic with them up there on the stage.

Someone asked me what I would have done if Keith had wanted me to give up my career when we got married. I replied without hesitation that I would not have found it possible to give up my career for anyone or anything. There would have been absolutely no contest. All the people who have surrounded me, from my parents onwards, have understood and accepted this. There is a terrible kind of ruthlessness in such a remark; for many, many years, music has come first and life second. Now, this position is about to be reversed and I feel that my profession, which I have served to my utmost limits, is giving me permission to make this reversal, and is in a curious way content to take second place in future. Whatever lessons I am about to learn from life, the ground has been prepared by my profession. All that I am, I owe to music; all that I will be, whatever it is, I shall also owe to music and to the musicians I have known.

In the evening, Elisabeth Speiser gave a party and some of us sat in her beautiful garden, talked as the light changed, and ate superb food.

A white dove fell into the fish pond; Keith helped to get it out and then held the bird gently in his hands, drying off the feathers with kitchen paper. When he had done what he could with it, he opened his hands, launching it into the air. In these final days, I feel very much like that bird. My young colleagues are dreading Saturday night; I have suggested to them that it won't be a sad occasion. My older colleagues and the management, although respecting my decision, are also sad. They are holding me, gently, as Keith held the captive bird. On Saturday night, the loving fingers will open and I shall be launched out into some unknown. The landscape – all the concerts and work to come – remains unchanged; but another element will enter; and I greet this new factor with a sense of anticipation. Perhaps all that will happen is the establishment of a more normal life pattern. If so, that will be for me the most exciting event, and I welcome it with open arms.

Wednesday   A large number of kind letters arriving from equally kind
14 July   people; how can I help but feel upheld, surrounded by so much gratitude and affection from friends and strangers alike?

When something comes to an end there is bound to be sadness. One feels it at the onset of Autumn, when children leave home; so many sorts of little 'deaths' which we all have to face.

Quite a lot of people believe I shall change my mind. If they really knew me, they would not entertain this thought for one moment, I'm far too Yorkshire and stubborn. There will be no flirting with 'opera in concert' for me. In a letter I received today, friends of the writer had comforted her with the remark, 'Oh! she'll go back to the stage – they always do!' Well, they always *don't*. Look at Ponselle and Nan Merriman, two singers who both did what I am about to do. In my case, musical life goes on; just because opera ceases, this doesn't mean *finis*! It has been an important third of my life, but there are still two more left, the concert and Lieder worlds, both of immense importance. There has been a tradition that when a singer can no longer appear on the stage, the field of Lieder can then provide a much *less* strenuous activity, as though to sing Lieder is in some way easier! The truth of the matter is very different. One doesn't put less into singing a recital programme; in my opinion it is the most testing sphere of all, the absolute pinnacle in terms of concentration, unbroken vocal and musical responsibility. It is easy to emphasise a point by movement on a stage. It is extremely difficult to make a similar emphasis when no movement is allowed.

I put my 'all' into my theatre work; I put the same 'all' into the concert platform, and although to the outward eye the singer is only standing there, the process is just as demanding in a different way as an opera, if not more so.

Performers come and go. The music is what matters – the music is for always.

Overleaf: 'Che farò senza Euridice . . .'

Woke up this morning with an extremely sore throat; very glum about it, and as the day passed didn't feel any better.

After a vocal warm-up in my dressing room a certain amount of voice appeared, but my chest felt raw and I think I was a bit feverish. Just before the curtain went up, I had a dreadful attack of coughing and called out for a glass of water which duly arrived and I was able to lubricate my throat, asking that the glass be kept handy at the prompt corner, in case I needed it.

It is a strange feeling to have one's concentration divided between concern for the music and concern for the instrument; I don't like it! To crown all, many people said the performance was stunning! I sometimes wonder whether the performer can judge in the slightest degree what is happening on stage.

By some extraordinary coincidence my throat specialist was in the audience and came round to see me afterwards. I told him I had been in difficulty and he took a quick look down my throat; he said it was very red. As he was staying in the area he decided to see me in the morning, which relieved my mind greatly. Mr Stein has cared for me superbly all my singing life, and took out my tonsils when I was nearly forty. It never occurred to me that he would think twice about it, since the wretched things were poisoning my system and I couldn't wait to get rid of them. But in retrospect, I suppose delving into the throat of a well-known singer is no joke! Anyway, he did a marvellous job on me and considers it an excellent thing that I don't have to consult him very often.

At 11 a.m., after taking the trouble to borrow the proper instruments from the local hospital, Mr Stein gave me the go-ahead to sing tomorrow, even though there was still some inflammation in the throat. The vocal chords were perfectly healthy. It is so often the case when singers complain of discomfort; the chords themselves are untouched and it is the

251

area which surrounds them which causes the trouble. Singers, being naturally sensitive about their throats, inevitably think the worst, that they will never sing again! But the vocal chords are extremely tough and can stand a great deal of punishment.

Mr Stein and his wife went off to their lunch engagement, leaving behind one relieved and grateful singer. He has given me some tablets to encourage the formation of mucus, which proved helpful as the day wore on and I coughed less and swallowed more easily.

A long telegram arrived all the way from Australia. Beloved John Copley will be thinking about me tomorrow and sent a loving message to tell me so.

We began to pack our clothes and gather together the books, papers, paraphernalia, collected over the past seven weeks, unable to believe we are actually going home tomorrow night. Home! My father is longing for us to be back and is all ready to cook a celebration lunch on Sunday.

Unable to get a train because of the strike, Anne, my friend from York, motored down and arrived around 4 p.m. It had been a long day for her cooped up in the car so we went for a walk by the sea before supper to refresh ourselves, and again afterwards, because it was such a pleasant evening. A clear sky and a strong breeze blowing; we hope for a fine day tomorrow. We went along to look at the sailing boats, tidily moored in the marina. It was a lovely sight. Gazing out over the sea, I thought of all the walks we've had here late at night, of the country lanes we've explored, of the friends we have visited, the happiness of the past months. It has been a richly varied and rewarding time.

My sister- and brother-in-law will have driven down to their son's house, and will be joining us, together with Andrew and Sue, for the final performance. Another great moment to share. My mother, wherever she is, will be throwing her cap in the air to think that her daughter is going to take things a little bit easier at last.

All the months since September seem to have telescoped, but nevertheless each moment has been significant. It has been one of the most, if not *the* most, interesting, fascinating, strenuous, daunting, and pressured seasons of my working life, and in some ways the most rewarding.

I shall not face tomorrow alone; as well as my family and closest friends, my colleagues and the staff of Glyndebourne are gathered round me. I could not ask for more. This last production has proved fulfilling beyond my greatest expectations; Peter and Ray have made it so. The place where I began my operatic career over twenty-five years ago is the place where I will end it. Mary Stuart's words, embroidered on a cloth of estate just before she died, express it exactly: 'In my end is my beginning'.

Saturday
17 July A perfect Summer morning; Brighton was *en fête* from an early hour, holiday makers pouring into the town. At 11 a.m. Bob, Cathy, and the film team arrived to take shots of us getting into the car; by then it was extremely hot, and after an hour's filming we were glad to get indoors and start preparing lunch, which had to be a proper meal on a performance day. We were working to an exact schedule; I knew the film crew wanted to use the hour well. We planned to finish lunch by 1 p.m. as both the drivers, Anne and Keith, were to start the journey home immediately after the opera was over and needed to rest. I hoped to sleep as well; I did, deeply, for nearly two hours. After a quick cup of tea, a final tidy round the flat, we were downstairs with the rest of the luggage and into the car on the dot of four o'clock. One of the cameramen rode in the back seat of our car to do some shots of the journey, a journey we have made countless times during the past weeks, almost always in glorious weather. We have seen the fields change in colour from green to bronze, the rolling contours

253

of the Downs stretching as far as the eye can see in one direction and in the other abruptly curtailed by a shining sea.

We drove into the town of Lewes to leave my books at the library. I have enjoyed my visits there; being even a temporary member of the library makes one 'belong' just a little. People in the town are friendly and smile as they pass in the street. It has the leisured air which most places in England possess once out of reach of the capital. Couldn't live anywhere else; this taste of sea and country air has been a joy, but London is the place for me.

Glanced around the library for the last time and thought how poor my existence would be without books; everywhere I go, when I'm away for any length of time, I join the local library. I should have kept all the tickets – they would make interesting reading!

We continued our journey, turning right up the lane to the house from Ringmer. I used to find that lane a long, steep pull on the occasions (very few!) when I overslept, missed the chorus bus, and had to walk to work from my digs at the end of the village. It was a thrill to turn into the final stretch and think what was waiting for me; the most fascinating job in the world. I felt exactly the same sort of thrill today; with all that has happened in between, the humble chorus member and the established singer are still the same person.

We arrived at the entrance and did a bit more filming, getting out of the car, moving down the corridor of the Opera House towards the pass door, through which I have always had unrestricted access. No more: after tonight that little door will look as forbidding to me as it no doubt does to members of the public.

My dressing room, filled to the brim with wonderful flowers, gifts, and messages, was soon at bursting-point, since the camera team squeezed in with all their equipment and proceeded to watch me clean my face and put on my make-up. I savoured the familiar speeding-up of the general tempo as curtain up approached;

people continuously streamed in and out. Guus Mostart came in to give me notes on the last performance; I asked him to do this each time we played because I needed to feel the discipline of constant correction, however slight. In a run of ten performances it is easy to take a different direction, quite unconsciously, with change and growth. I wanted to develop, but only within the framework Peter had laid down for us. Guus has been extremely helpful and very patient, encouraging me to make adjustments, discouraging me if certain moves got out of hand. He will be in charge of the touring company's performances later in the year.

Geoffrey Gilbertson, Front of House Manager, came in to tell me a lovely story about the first man in the queue for returns for tonight's performance, who had staked his claim at midnight on Friday by placing a stuffed dog with a note in its mouth by the box office window. The note informed anyone who was interested that he was representing the owner asleep in his car not far away, and if anyone objected to the method of queuing, they should wake up the said owner, who would then come and stand through the night in person. Otherwise, the owner would be there early in the morning, which he was, at crack of dawn. His virtue was rewarded because at 7.30 a.m. the first return came through and he got it!

In spite of film cameras dodging in and out of my dressing room and along the corridor, milling people, a general air of excitement, I was surprised by my own inner calm. Unlike the day of the final performance at the Coliseum, when I had been highly emotional until entering the theatre, I had wakened this morning feeling absolutely in control, and this continued.

Curtain up – we launched into the performance – the theatre was very hot – Elizabeth Gale singing like the angel she is – also the chorus – the Hades scene safely over – Elisabeth Speiser in her best voice. The final moment with the chorus, just before the end of the first part, was the most vulnerable for me. This is the

255

scene which moved me so deeply, the first time we tried it all those weeks ago in the early days of rehearsal, where we all exchange hand clasps. Each time we have played this scene it has been unbearably beautiful, and I knew if I was going to break, it would be here. The sound my young colleagues made as they gathered round me on the stage was out of this world; we played it together for the last time before the public in a theatre, and I shall never forget it as long as I live. We have exchanged more than hand clasps; we have touched each other with infinite tenderness and respect; we have looked deeply into each other's eyes and souls; we have shared and communicated something indescribably precious. If any moment could sum up the beauty of my whole theatre experience it would be this one. And all it involves is the touch of the human hand.

The profession survives because there is always remarkable talent emerging; up through the ranks come the great singers of the next generations. In some way, I felt all the hope, dedication, love, which I have brought to the stage being passed through my hands to those young people; in return they have given me their respect and their affection. I hope they have learned from me as I have certainly learned from them. We all came through this moment with a glorious joy, regardless of the tears in many eyes.

The interval went by quickly, as it always does; in no time at all the half-hour was called, and I got dressed again.

The second part is short, although highly charged emotionally, and by the time 'Che farò' is finished I am glad to have the final happy dance scene in which to come down to earth again.

The curtain fell. We had given our all, and the audience had given just as much back to us.

Wave after wave of appreciation swept across the pit towards us. There was foot stamping and cheering, everyone on their feet, and the slow 'Continental' hand clap one hears abroad, but very rarely in this country.

258

The sense of exhilaration and joy I had felt all day rose to bursting-point as the love of everyone in the building surrounded me. What a moment! What a way to make my exit!

Brian Dickie came on stage and began to speak. I had Ray next to me and his hand held mine in a fiercely protective grip as he supported me during the words Brian spoke; and *such* words. Brian was obviously moved, and sad and dignified, at the same time expressing, as did John Tooley, gladness for me. I loved the way he spoke; even more moving than the words was the way his voice broke a little as he strove to say what he and the company felt about my work, and the marvellous significance of that work beginning and ending on the Glyndebourne stage.

Then he presented me with a letter, beautifully bound, from Hector Berlioz to Pauline Viardot, written during the time of their collaboration over *Orfeo* in Paris in 1859, a perfect gift and appropriate in so many different ways. In between more curtain calls, the chorus presented me with my lyre; an engraved plate had been attached to it between the end of the performance and the speeches, and it read: *To Janet, with love and admiration from your chorus, Glyndebourne 1982. My* chorus.

During the final scene of the opera when the gods descend to bless us, Jove indicates that I must return the golden lyre which was given to me for my journey to the Underworld, to help me tame the Furies; he commands me to hand it back to Apollo. As I walked across with it cradled in my arms, the final testing moment arrived. The fleeting thought came to me: Are you really handing back this symbol of your art with a pure intention? Are you truly relinquishing the power you have been lent? And back came my answer: 'I am.' I did not know then that my lyre, and all it means, was going to be returned to me, and returned by these marvellous young singers, who had watched me struggle with its weight, discard it for the lighter one, and take it up again because somehow I had to use the original. A symbol of an ending, and now, through their gift, the symbol of a

Final curtain: with Elisabeth Speiser, Raymond Leppard, Peter Hall, and Elizabeth Gale

new beginning. Nothing happens by accident, and it was no accident that the lyre was both taken from me and returned again tonight.

The curtain fell for the last time and I went back to my dressing room to see Joan, Geoff, Andy and Sue, Julia, Anne and Keith, who, with four special friends, Elizabeth and John Moore, Bill Corlett and Bryn Ellis, made up my 'family' group.

The cameras were busy but I didn't really notice what was going on. Zoë was also taking pictures; many familiar faces, handshakes and hugs.

Eventually, Keith and I got away and went over to the house to say a quiet good-bye to George and Mary Christie, the people who perhaps sacrifice more than anyone else in the amount of time, energy, privacy, and heart's-blood they pour out upon Glyndebourne. Another moment to cherish, although we will meet often in the future in other circumstances.

I went back to my dressing room, checked to see nothing was left behind, and walked out of the theatre by the door at the back of the stage.

Grouped around the door of the bar were many members of the chorus and staff. They were waiting for me, calling out as we passed; they began to applaud and went on applauding as we reached the tennis court, and walked on towards the car park. I turned around and waved, and walked backwards waving, with my lyre held up for them to see. Suddenly they broke into song, and the strains of 'For she's a jolly good fellow' rang out, until we disappeared from sight.

I opened the car door, sniffed the scent of tobacco plants, got inside and fastened my seat belt.

We drove off into the night.

Appendix

Janet Baker:
The Operatic Roles
COMPILED BY PAUL HIRSCHMAN

1956   Glyndebourne, chorus
Oxford University Opera Club: THE SECRET (Smetana) *Rosa*

1957   Glyndebourne, chorus
Ingestre Hall: DIDO AND AENEAS (Purcell) *Second Witch*

1958   Morley College: ORFEO (Gluck) *Orfeo*

1959   Bath: DIDO AND AENEAS (Purcell) *Sorceress*
Hampton Court: DIDO AND AENEAS (Purcell) *Sorceress*
Handel Opera Society, Sadler's Wells: RODELINDA (Handel)
    Eduige
Wexford: LA GAZZA LADRA (Rossini) *Pippo*

1960   BBC Broadcast: THE MIDSUMMER MARRIAGE (Tippett) *Sosostris*

1961   Barber Institute, Birmingham: DIDO AND AENEAS (Purcell) *Dido*

1962   Barber Institute, Birmingham: TAMERLANO (Handel) *Irene*
English Opera Group, Drottningholm: DIDO AND AENEAS
    (Purcell) *Dido*
English Opera Group, Aldeburgh: DIDO AND AENEAS (Purcell)
    Dido
Handel Opera Society, Sadler's Wells: JEPHTHA (Handel) *Storge*
Handel Opera Society, Liège: JEPHTHA (Handel) *Storge*

1963   English Opera Group, Edinburgh: THE BEGGAR'S OPERA (Gay)
    Polly

1964   Barber Institute, Birmingham: ARIODANTE (Handel) *Ariodante*
English Opera Group, Russian tour: THE RAPE OF LUCRETIA
    (Britten) *Lucretia*; ALBERT HERRING (Britten) *Nancy*
English Opera Group tour: ALBERT HERRING (Britten) *Nancy*

1965   Barber Institute, Birmingham: HIPPOLYTE ET ARICIE (Rameau)
    Phaedra
Oxford Playhouse: HIPPOLYTE ET ARICIE (Rameau) *Phaedra*

267

1966   Royal Opera House, Covent Garden: A MIDSUMMER NIGHT'S
       DREAM (Britten) *Hermia*
       Barber Institute, Birmingham: ORLANDO (Handel) *Orlando*
       Glyndebourne: DIDO AND AENEAS (Purcell) *Dido*
       Handel Opera Society, Sadler's Wells: ORLANDO (Handel)
       Orlando
       Albert Hall: THE TROJANS, Part I (Berlioz) *Cassandra*
       English Opera Group tour: THE RAPE OF LUCRETIA (Britten)
       Lucretia
       New York concert performance: ANNA BOLENA (Donizetti)
       Smeaton
       New York concert performance: SERSE (Handel) *Amastris*

1967   BBC Broadcast: LA CLEMENZA DI TITO (Mozart) *Sextus*
       Scottish Opera: COSI FAN TUTTE (Mozart) *Dorabella*

1968   San Francisco concert performance: ORFEO (Gluck) *Orfeo*
       Barber Institute, Birmingham: ADMETO (Handel) *Alcestis*
       Aldeburgh: HERCULES (Handel) *Dejanira*

1969   San Diego concert performance: ORFEO (Gluck) *Orfeo*
       Scottish Opera: COSI FAN TUTTE (Mozart) *Dorabella*
       Scottish Opera: THE TROJANS (Berlioz) *Dido*
       Royal Opera House, Covent Garden: THE TROJANS (Berlioz) *Dido*
       English Opera Group, Sadler's Wells: THE RAPE OF LUCRETIA
       (Britten) *Lucretia*

1970   Glyndebourne: LA CALISTO (Cavalli) *Diana*
       Aldeburgh: THE RAPE OF LUCRETIA (Britten) *Lucretia*

1971   BBC 2: OWEN WINGRAVE (Britten) *Kate*
       Scottish Opera: DER ROSENKAVALIER (Strauss) *Octavian*
       Glyndebourne: LA CALISTO (Cavalli) *Diana*
       Albert Hall: LA CALISTO, concert performance; *Diana*
       English National Opera, Coliseum: THE CORONATION OF
       POPPEA (Monteverdi) *Poppea*
       English National Opera, Coliseum: THE DAMNATION OF FAUST
       (Berlioz) *Marguerite*

1972   Glyndebourne: IL RITORNO D'ULISSE IN PATRIA (Monteverdi)
       Penelope
       Albert Hall: IL RITORNO D'ULISSE IN PATRIA, concert
       performance; *Penelope*

268

Scottish Opera: THE TROJANS (Berlioz) *Dido*
Royal Opera House, Covent Garden: THE TROJANS (Berlioz) *Dido*

1973 BBC Broadcast: TAMERLANO (Handel) *Tamerlano*
Royal Opera House, Covent Garden: OWEN WINGRAVE (Britten)
Kate
Glyndebourne: IL RITORNO D'ULISSE IN PATRIA (Monteverdi)
Penelope
English National Opera, Coliseum: MARY STUART (Donizetti)
Mary Stuart

1974 Royal Opera House, Covent Garden: LA CLEMENZA DI TITO
(Mozart) *Vitellia*
Aldeburgh: SAVITRI (Holst) *Savitri*; DIDO AND AENEAS (Purcell)
Dido
English National Opera, Coliseum: MARY STUART (Donizetti)
Mary Stuart (BBC concert performance only)

1975 Royal Opera House, Covent Garden: LA CLEMENZA DI TITO
(Mozart) *Vitellia*
English National Opera, Coliseum: MARY STUART (Donizetti)
Mary Stuart
Scottish Opera: ARIADNE AUF NAXOS (Strauss) *The Composer*
Scottish Opera: COSI FAN TUTTE (Mozart) *Dorabella*
BBC Broadcast: ARIODANTE (Handel) *Ariodante*

1976 Royal Opera House, Covent Garden: LA CLEMENZA DI TITO
(Mozart) *Vitellia* (Production then taken on tour to La Scala,
Milan.)
Royal Opera House, Covent Garden: TROILUS AND CRESSIDA
(Walton) *Cressida*
Recording only: I CAPULETI E I MONTECCHI (Bellini) *Romeo*

1977 English National Opera, Coliseum: WERTHER (Massenet)
Charlotte (two seasons)
Scottish Opera: ARIADNE AUF NAXOS (Strauss) *The Composer*

1978 Royal Opera House, Covent Garden: IDOMENEO (Mozart)
Idamantes
Recording only: BÉATRICE ET BÉNÉDICT (Berlioz) *Béatrice*
Aix-en-Provence: DIDO AND AENEAS (Purcell) *Dido*
Albert Hall: ORFEO (Gluck) concert performance; *Orfeo*

269

Albert Hall: OEDIPUS REX (Stravinsky) concert performance; *Jocasta*

Scottish Opera: DIDO AND AENEAS (Purcell) *Dido*; SAVITRI (Holst) *Savitri*

1979   Royal Opera House, Covent Garden: IDOMENEO (Mozart) *Idamantes*

Scottish Opera: ORFEO (Gluck) *Orfeo*

English National Opera, Coliseum: JULIUS CAESAR (Handel) *Julius Caesar*

1980   BBC Broadcast: IMENEO (Handel) *Tirinthus*

English National Opera, Liverpool: JULIUS CAESAR (Handel) *Julius Caesar*

1981   English National Opera, Coliseum: JULIUS CAESAR (Handel) *Julius Caesar*

Spitalfields Festival: DIDO AND AENEAS (Purcell) *Dido*

Royal Opera House, Covent Garden: ALCESTE (Gluck) *Alceste*

1982   English National Opera, Coliseum: MARY STUART (Donizetti) *Mary Stuart*

Glyndebourne: ORFEO (Gluck) *Orfeo*

Albert Hall: ORFEO (Gluck) *Orfeo*